HIDDEN GEMS *of* ASIA

EVERY PIECE TELLS A STORY

HIDDEN GEMS OF ASIA
Every piece tells a story

ISBN 978-988-18094-2-1

Published in Hong Kong by Haven Books Limited
www.havenbooksonline.com

Design & cover direction: Candace Campos
Layout designer: Katie Kwan
Design assistant: Eman Lam

HIDDEN GEMS *of* ASIA

EVERY PIECE TELLS A STORY

Tara Jenkins
Karen Pittar

HAVEN
BOOKS

Contents

PREFACE

HIDDEN GEMS OF ASIA celebrates the style and vision of ten designers who have been quietly setting new standards in modern jewellery design in Asia. They are taste makers; their loyal followers are discerning, fashion-forward women who have come to expect original beauty and thoughtful craftsmanship in each piece they collect. Writers Karen Pittar and Tara Jenkins have drawn out the personal stories and intimate sources of inspiration behind each designer's creative evolution. In Hong Kong, they sat down with Sandra d'Auriol, Sin Sin, Trini Tambu, Tayma Page Allies, Sandrine Clayton and Toni Patrizio. They spoke, too, with Cindy Chao in Taiwan, Dora Tam in Macau, Wynn Wynn Ong in the Philippines, and Jean-François Fichot in Bali. The resulting chapters reveal the designers' wholly unique approaches to their craft. These chapters also reveal fundamental traits which make the designers who they are:

10 unconventional creative minds. The designers in this book have a cerebral connection with jewellery. They understand where their art is coming from, and each has developed a certain way of approaching design. As a result, their respective work has its own distinctive hallmark look.

10 passionate advocates for centuries-old craftsmanship. They employ people whose artisanal skills have been honed for generations, from hand forged metalwork, engraving, beading, knotting and inlaid gems, to cloisonné, wirework, traditional silversmithing, jade relief carving and intricate stone cutting.

10 devotees of nature's beauty. While most walk past everyday wonders, these designers study the delicacy of a butterfly, the curves of a leaf or the texture of bark. They are inspired by rolling ocean waves, morning dew or a spider's web. They then turn nature's work into wearable art, and the process with which they accomplish this is magical. Their jewellery is tactile and organic, rather than traditionally beautiful.

10 trendsetters in both style and technique. Pioneering new methods such as 360° settings, or the mixing of precious gems with unexpected materials such as natural fibres or wood, they flout their industry's conventions in the pursuit of breathtaking results.

10 citizens of the world, who bring a rich mix of cultural references to their craft. Living and working in Asia, they are inspired by the lush topography and diverse traditions of the East. Memories of childhoods spent on other continents—in Africa or Europe or South America—permeate their design aesthetic. This melding of global influences shows in often astounding choices in shape, colour and materials.

Nothing thrills quite like discovering beauty. Our ten hidden gems make it their life's work to give us that pleasure, with every new piece they conceive and create. We celebrate their success.

Dania Shawwa Abuali
Publisher, Haven Books

SANDRA d'AURIOL

*"I am best known for my original use of jade —
my work is about creating timeless pieces that have
meaning, and using materials in unexpected ways.
When a stone is beautiful, its soul speaks."*

My early childhood was spent between a rather old-fashioned colonial life in India, where my family had been for generations, and a much more relaxed life of Ibizan summers in the sixties and seventies. These were the places where my love for jewellery began. For me it was a fascination from the age of four; I wore as many bangles and rings as I could put on!

The visual passion I have for all things must have been formed in those early years; it gave me a broad view of mixing materials, colours and symbolism, which have remained the hallmarks of my work today. I love the patina and texture of things; a piece of ancient turquoise or jade, the worn softness of Rajasthani silver, the warmth of hand-beaten gold, the crisp coolness of Qing jade, the mirror-like quality of old diamonds.

Although today my designs are far more sophisticated, there is always a clear reminder of the nature of the stone. I often return to the simplicity of putting a beautiful pendant on a cord; the reminder that it all started with twine—the earliest jewellery worn by man. The stone doesn't have to be valuable; it has to have soul. Every stone is nature at its most fundamental, and artists throughout the millennia have simply tried to showcase its beauty. Colour, texture, contrasting materials, ancient and modern, classic, ethnic, and a dash of the unexpected—sometimes my pieces are quite spare and delicate, and other times they are profuse, organic and abundant, just like nature itself. Many are designed specifically to represent one's family, like my 'family portrait' bracelet, or the charm collection necklace. I think it is important to personalize things as much as possible, especially on one's everyday or commemorative pieces.

Although I fiddled with jewellery design for many years, it was only really in 1997 that I took the plunge and committed myself to putting my name on my own collection. This coincided with a growing feeling of wanting to give back to the world around me, so when I started my business it was with the idea that 30% of my retail price would go towards charities like the Child Welfare Scheme, benefiting the children of Nepal. In 2007, my husband agreed that all proceeds from my business could go to fund different social and environmental projects. This has been the greatest of gifts, allowing me to get involved in a much wider range of projects, and giving a lot of meaning to my life. In my mind, jewellery is a necessity, but in reality it is a luxury. So it only makes it more special that when one spoils oneself, one spoils others.

I try as much as possible to use individual craftsmen, encouraging them to keep their ancient skills and crafts alive, and to use sustainable materials. The coral I use today is old stock I bought years ago, I would not dream of ordering it again today. It seems so sad to continue ripping up one of nature's most beautiful landscapes to make things that only a few will enjoy, and will often end up in a safe! I will only be proud of myself when I have created a collection of jewellery using truly sustainable materials, and made it just as precious to those who wear it.

Of course Asia has always been my main inspiration. My grandmother collected jade before the Second World War; she lost most of it during the occupation of Indonesia, but that innate love for the stone must have been passed to me. When I moved to Hong Kong in 1983 the first thing I bought was a small carved Qing dynasty dragon, which I gave to my husband on our second date; it still sits on his desk today. Indeed, it was discovering jade in Hong Kong that inspired me. My first designs were really just beautiful jade pieces suspended on a cord. I am especially drawn to the beautiful Shang Dynasty jades carved over 4000 years ago; they are as contemporary today as they were then.

I often wonder, who was the first person to pick up a shell, a feather, a stone, and put it on a piece of twine, twisting it around their neck, their wrist? That first piece of jewellery—why did they create it? Was it because they loved the piece and wanted to keep it with them? I still have that primal sense about the jewellery I make; I feel there is an element of this organic rawness in all my work. I love found things, driftwood, stone, shell—nature at its most beautiful. And nothing could be more representative of our world or culture than the circle, not just the visual but also its symbolic side. If I had to live with one piece of jewellery for the rest of my life, it would be a simple circular band, because you never tire of it. —SdA

CLOCKWISE FROM TOP: *Carved antique horn necklace; Tahitian pearl, jade and netsuke necklace; matching jade bracelet; antique Qing jade phoenix and diamond earrings*

ANCIENT

"The craftsmanship is stunning in its simplicity; the relatively heavy jade is suspended from a delicate piece of gold that expertly follows the contours of the carving."

Nowhere is Sandra d'Auriol's love of contrast more apparent than in the design of her exquisite Tahitian Pearl and Netsuke Necklace. Twenty gleaming South Sea baroque pearls, stunning in all their imperfection, are strung between nephrite jade, champagne diamond links and hardwood Japanese netsuke carvings.

The intricate netsuke carvings were originally part of another bead necklace, to which d'Auriol felt an immediate attraction. Netsuke are miniature sculptures dating from Japan in the 17th century, which traditionally hung from the sash of a man's kimono. "My husband bought me some perfect round grey pearls, but they felt too dressy for how I live and wear my jewellery. I asked him if he'd mind if I changed them for baroque pearls — I love their tactile quality, each one with its own personality. To contrast the luminescence of the pearls, I created an organic-shaped link of nephrite and added a pave diamond clasp to bring a little contrast to the opaqueness of the nephrite. I chose champagne-coloured diamonds rather than white because I wanted a more casual, tonal look. I had always loved pearls but found them a bit formal for my lifestyle; now I can wear them, but this remains a more sophisticated winter piece." To make the necklace more personal, d'Auriol used the netsuke beads, along with jade carvings, to represent the Chinese zodiac signs of her husband and children. The accompanying bracelet is a simple combination of nephrite and champagne diamond links. "I used a different type of nephrite on the bracelet; it is highly polished and greener than the one used on the necklace. I wanted the necklace to look more 'woody'."

D'Auriol's curious mix of sophistication with the raw and organic is perfectly showcased in the antique jade and diamond phoenix earrings. The jade dates from the Qing Dynasty, and depicts a phoenix with a sweeping tail amongst the fronds, flowers and leaves of a garden; the phoenix was traditionally the symbol of the Empress. To give definition and add a modern twist to the piece, d'Auriol has placed a tiny sparkling diamond in the eye of the phoenix, and diamonds across the top of each earring. The craftsmanship is stunning in its simplicity; the relatively heavy jade is suspended from a delicate piece of gold that expertly follows the contours of the carving. "I used grey gold for this piece; it's very industrial, and I love the way the precious champagne diamonds contrast against the matte brushed gold. I believe the jade would have been originally sewn onto clothes or coats as decoration."

The contrast of ancient and modern is also the defining characteristic in d'Auriol's antique horn necklace, which portrays two figures in a classical Chinese garden, complete with pagodas and a beautiful blossom tree. The horn is carved on both sides, but has an unusual beauty in that it is creamy grey on one side, and brown on the reverse. To bring the antique piece up to date and give it extra interest, d'Auriol has edged the horn with matte grey gold, and cleverly strung black leather cord through diamond-studded struts. "I loved the antique horn and didn't want to interfere with the material itself, so I made the setting around the edge like a bezel. I cut the cord in several places so it sticks out at an unusual angle, but I have worn this piece so much it needs to be restrung!"

Natural
BEAUTY

"Most people think amber is only orangey-brown, but it actually comes in a host of colours — so wild, so fun, so completely natural."

Sandra d'Auriol has always had a penchant for beautiful diamonds, like most women; but today she is drawn to stones that reflect nature's raw beauty. High on her list is the phosphorescent splendor of the Australian opal, the mesmerising hero stone of her avant-garde Black Opal Ring. "I don't think we can design anything more beautiful than what we find in nature; I look at stones and wonder at how extraordinary the natural world is. I am mad about opals and moonstones, they are so connective, so magical—the depth, the subtle interplay of colours. You can never see to the bottom of an opal, it's like a hologram. I particularly love this stone because it is completely natural; many opals have quartz or clear plastic placed on top as protection."

The stone's attraction lies in its extraordinary mix of blues, greens and turquoises, constantly shimmering beneath the surface. Despite its vivid colouring, the huge stone used in the ring is known as a black opal— because it is so dark—and d'Auriol has chosen two rows of sophisticated, brilliant red rubies, set into yellow gold, to encircle the central opal. "I had such a strong intuition to put the opal with the rubies, I didn't realize it at the time, but rubies are very grounding stones, and opals are very chaotic. If you are feeling chaotic, don't wear an opal! It's a hugely powerful ring, I find it very energizing, but you need to feel good to wear it!"

Continuing the theme of vivid colour is d'Auriol's asymmetrical necklace of candy-hued amber and jade. This necklace is strung with over twenty pieces of

different coloured amber, opaque and translucent, and is cleverly contrasted with four pieces of carved jade. "I bought the amber piece by piece in China; I thought it was all so luscious, the peachy pinks, the grassy greens. Most people think amber is only orangey-brown, but it actually comes in a host of colours. I thought it was so wild, so fun, so completely natural!" D'Auriol used a thick cord to string the pieces together, and she edged the creamy striped jade in 22-carat gold. The carvings on the larger piece are of bats, which symbolize longevity. "I designed the big piece of jade to be worn at the side of the neck; it's nice to have the contrast of stone against the amber. I love the unexpected." The necklace looks hefty, but thanks to the the naturally light-weight amber it is surprisingly delicate to wear.

It is apt that d'Auriol has chosen the harmony cloud pattern to grace her stylish nephrite bangles; tradition says the pattern symbolizes harmony between humans and nature. Her fascination with shape is also markedly apparent, as the bangles have been deliberately designed to be oval, rather than round: "The actual shape of your arm is oval, so it makes more sense to have an oval bangle—round-shaped bangles of this size don't sit that comfortably on your wrist." In an unusual twist, the 22-carat gold has a scalloped edge, which cleverly accentuates the nephrite carving. "The gold has character, you feel it has been made by hand. These bangles could have been made two thousand years ago and they would have looked exactly the same; they are timeless, still fresh."

Found OBJECTS

Invited to a charity evening themed around Chinese Explorers, Sandra d'Auriol had planned to wear an elegant grey Chinese evening coat. Casting around for the perfect piece of jewellery, she felt none of her necklaces were large or significant enough to offset the coat. "Everything was too small, it looked lost. I wanted to create a piece that felt ancient and had a bit of fantasy to it." The result was her fantastic Jade and Rope Necklace offset with tiny diamonds, which gives the piece contrast and a dainty lightness. The top piece of antique jade is a creamy green with hints of brown; it features a dragon and was an old belt buckle—d'Auriol had originally planned to use it as a choker. The creamy brown bottom piece is carved with an ornate phoenix, claws and wings outstretched, and both are enhanced by d'Auriol's trademark grey gold studded with tiny diamonds. To further unite the two jade pieces, both the dragon and the phoenix have diamond-studded eyes. "It's perfectly balanced because the top piece is the dragon, symbolizing the emperor, and the bottom piece is the phoenix—or empress! I'd had the jade pieces for a long time and had set them with diamonds, they were sitting there waiting to be made, so I got out my cord, and put it together for the evening. I love old jewellery that has a history to it; you feel the age when you touch it. The Chinese have a saying that if you are wearing a piece of jade and it breaks, it has broken to protect you from something else!"

D'Auriol has cleverly merged two great cultures in her Dragon Jade Necklace. India and China, which have both played a significant role in her life, have been seamlessly brought together in a powerful combination of carved jade, coloured diamonds, and iridescent slices of pearl. The purples, greens, browns, greys, aubergines and flecked green of the pearls highlight the fabulous piece of jade, which is intricately carved with a huge, mystical dragon. What makes the piece even more unique is the careful placement of nineteen tiny teardrop diamonds: "I love Indian diamonds, they are my favourite because they are like dewdrops; they come in these amazing natural shapes, some of them are even triangular! I'm not crazy about new cut diamonds, I like the old cuts. The ones I chose for this piece all have a yellow gold hue, they're all tonal. I used the pearl slices because I wanted something quite metallic to go with the jade, rather than use another stone. Using the pearls is more unexpected, more unusual; the colours that range through them perfectly complement the jade."

With her Stingray, Diamond and Jade Cuff, d'Auriol demonstrates yet again her love of contrast, and her determination to source unusual and beautiful materials. "I had a huge collection of these Qing dynasty jades that I had built up over the years, more than 150 pieces. They are so beautiful, so fragile." Set against the wood, the jade is protected and its delicate pale green finds a striking contrast in the warmth of the ebony. The velvety jade used dates from the Xing Dynasty, and depicts two men in a garden; the tiny diamonds surrounding the carving soften the piece, giving the jade an ethereal glow. The shape of the diamonds perfectly echoes the pattern of the stingray, and the colours all tone beautifully.

D'Auriol has chosen nephrite, diamonds and white gold for the second cuff, lending the piece an ancient, earthy feel: "Nephrite is opaque and heavy, but the stone holds such mystery—you get a great density in nephrite, as you do in jade. One of the themes running through my jewellery is the strength of stone, combined with delicate dainty materials such as diamonds. It's a wonderful opposite, and here the diamonds look so pure against the nephrite. It is bold simplicity, sitting alongside the organic."

"I love cuffs, they are so strong. If I want a sophisticated look I wear one beautiful piece, and a cuff is strong enough to wear on its own. I would only wear a lovely pair of stud earrings with it. Cuffs are always a statement. They go back to primitive times; it's such a sculptural form of adornment."

"I love old jewellery that has a history to it; you feel the age when you touch it."

Family PORTRAIT

"Wearing this bracelet is like wearing a portrait of your life, and this is so much more the direction we're going in. Everyone wants something personal, something that is uniquely theirs."

There is a tradition in the d'Auriol household that gifts between the children—be they birthday, Christmas or anniversary—must be hand-made by the giver. This was the inspiration behind d'Auriol's striking Family Portrait bracelet, which is one of her best-selling designs. Beautifully pared back, the bracelet can be made in wood, white or black resin, and is held together by 18-carat yellow gold links, set with ornate coral (the bracelet is no longer available in coral) or turquoise carvings.

"I love creating things for people that are personal, and I wanted to make a bracelet that could be worn at different stages of life; as easily at 30 as at 80." Each of the carvings is a unique symbol that represents a member of the family. While the majority of the carvings are signs from the Chinese zodiac, d'Auriol will occasionally use her creative instincts to design alternative symbols. "I made a beautiful bracelet for a woman who didn't have children, but she had a collection of amazing African masks, which I had copied into the coral in those days." Another bracelet had flowers for each season; and yet another included the Chinese characters for virtues one client was trying to bring into her life. So the bracelets can depict more than family; they can be symbolic of their owner's life journey.

"My latest pieces are much more significant to me. Wearing this bracelet is like wearing a portrait of your life, and this is the direction we're going in—everyone wants something personal, something that is uniquely theirs. I was always so completely crazy about jewellery. From when I was small, I recognized my mother's friends from the rings, necklaces, bracelets they wore. I knew who wore what—it identified who they were. I feel similarly about houses now, so many people use interior designers and stylists; I miss walking into a house and getting an immediate impression of what someone is like."

"Your own sense of style is so important; I revel in the fact my girlfriends are all so different and confident in their tastes. When they come to my shows they stand in front of the table and I let them go first, I don't try to influence them. When they choose a piece it's like finding a bit of themselves. People walk in and say they love something, I will often make changes to their piece ensure it suits them, is in proportion, or I might add in little details that make it more personal—it gives me so much pleasure to be able to create something truly meaningful for somebody."

Resin, gold and coral Family Portrait bracelets

Circle of LIFE

Sandra d'Auriol loves big rings and each one she designs is imbued with her own sense of style and comfort. "I couldn't bear the fact when you were wearing a large ring you wanted to take it off all the time because it was uncomfortable, or if you shook someone's hand it would crush your fingers!" With this in mind, she set about designing statement rings, which are cut in at the sides to make them comfortable to wear all day, while still having a striking, large top. The Planetary Collection ring features an impressive pink rubelite, orbited by three tiers of zingy orange sapphires, with a piping in the centre of grey gold. "The grey gold is so understated, and rather sober, contrasting beautifully with the outrageous colour of the sapphires and the rubelite. I didn't want a pave look, I wanted circular bands reminding me of the planets, hence the name. I have done them in wonderful different mixes of colour."

The Dragon and Pig rings both feature ornate carvings offset by a circle of tiny sparkling diamonds. Set into d'Auriol's signature brushed 18-carat yellow gold, the pig and blossom tree are carved into an antique brown nut: "It's so unexpected to see brown in the centre of a ring. The Chinese loved carving onto little things like walnuts, and they used to string them on cord as symbols of good luck. They are beautiful objects, but in today's world the challenge is finding a way to use them, hence the modern design of the ring! I love things that incorporate meaning, and have a hidden secret." The dragon is carved into coral, and is set into ebony and 18-carat white gold. The gold edging has been distressed to give texture and interest to the piece, and echoes the scales on the dragon's back. "The dragon is the emperor but also represents a nobility of spirit; you would give it to someone who has chosen to follow a certain path in life."

Forming part of her most recent collection are the sheet diamond rings—a delicate design of flat diamonds. They have a breathtaking, icy beauty; the stone literally comes to life on the hand. The delicately faceted sheet diamonds are from India and come in a variety of mesmerizing and delicate hues, from pale champagne to off white. The surface of each diamond is flecked with a multitude of colours and imperfections, inside you can see black and gold flecks and cracks running through the stone. "The stones are mined and cut into sheets. I kept the natural shape because of the organic feel, it reminds me of picking a pebble up on the beach. I have captured a piece of nature! Most of my jewellery has a softness about it, I don't like hard shapes. Even if the piece is very bold there is a tactileness about it, you want to reach out and touch it." The central stone is so impressive it needs only a subtle, low-key setting, so d'Auriol has used an industrial grey gold. "I love it because it tends to melt into my colour range. I don't want my settings to be garish, although they are very strong. Sometimes you don't want to wear an in-your-face piece, you want something which is light and delicate and goes with everything, but still has a personality of its own."

One of d'Auriol's best selling designs is the stunning black resin and diamond Double Happiness ring. In keeping with her love of contrast, d'Auriol has chosen to combine lustrous black resin with tiny white diamonds, depicting the Chinese symbol for Double Happiness. "I slightly manipulated the character to give it a more modern and edgy feel, and part of its impact is its horizontal—rather than vertical—setting." The ring looks equally fabulous in d'Auriol's white resin setting, and can either be worn to a black-tie event or simply every day with jeans and t-shirt!

"Nothing could be more representative of our world or culture than the circle – not just the visual but also its symbolic side."

Double Happiness ring

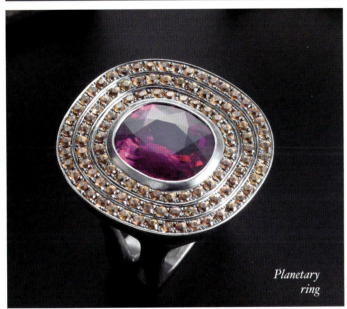

Planetary ring

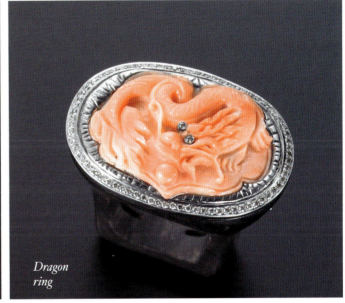

Dragon ring

Sheet diamond ring

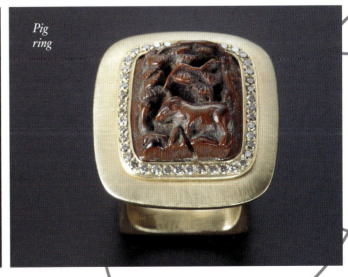

Pig ring

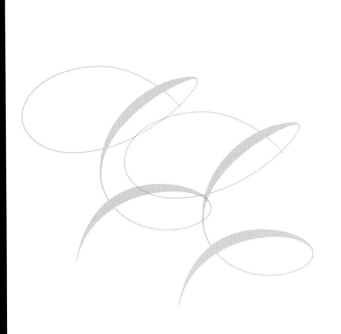

CINDY CHAO

"I have endeavoured to become a true master of art jewellery; I want people to feel that owning a piece of my Art Jewel collection is like possessing miniature architecture."

I was raised in an environment where art and architecture were a huge part of my life. My grandfather was a Taiwanese architect of ancient Chinese palace structures in the 20th century. He created graceful Buddhist temples now classified as historical monuments; he often took me on-site to watch his designs come to life. My father, an art sculptor, also played a significant role in my childhood. While he worked on sculptures in his studios, he used to hand me clay and would encourage me to observe my surroundings, and then teach me to sculpt what I saw. Thus my grandfather inspired me, whilst my father shaped me.

I had always planned to become an interior designer, as architecture had been such a strong childhood interest of mine, but my mother encouraged me to pursue jewellery design. One day she asked for my help in redesigning a ruby ring and, in shaping it directly from wax molding, I fell in love with the creation. Seeing the impact my creation had on the woman who eventually wore it, sparked a lifelong passion: to use my love of sculpture and architecture concepts. It was a challenge to incorporate architectural concepts into my designs, but as a result, even today, every Art Jewel is intricately designed and crafted, complexly layered with diamonds, and can be admired from all possible angles.

What sets me apart from my peers is the way my design ethos has developed over the years. I personally carve out wax moldings for each piece—a jewellery-making process that is rarely seen today—and by using this as a foundation, I have been able to exercise creative control over an evolution of structural pieces with the designs defined by intricate layering and three-dimensional curvatures.

Starting from the past, my focus towards my avant-garde Art Jewel concept first shifted in 2007. When I initially changed design direction, many of my existing clients were unable to accept the thrust of my new creations. During that time, mostly black and white diamonds were utilized to reflect my sombre mood but I stayed true to my creative concept. A wider spectrum of colours was finally explored when my work began to be recognized and accepted internationally by collectors from around the world.

Most of my most original inspirations tend to come from unlikely sources, and as an artist, I travel the world to gain new experiences to widen my creative horizons. Being Taiwanese, then having spent a few years in New York, and now being back in Taiwan again, has left me eternally fascinated with cultural conflicts and the merging of East and West; I love to fuse elements from different sources to create a unique piece of jewellery that is more than meets the eye.

Ultimately, I believe an exceptional jeweller should have an acute sense of perception, an undying passion for design, boundless imagination and creativity, as well as a determined drive to excel. I have endeavoured to become a jewellery artist, with an ongoing ambition to create new pieces with designs and craftsmanship that surpasses any previous work. Since all my Art Jewels are custom-made and unique, each design has its own challenges to overcome. The most difficult part for me is finding the right balance between reaching for the stars and facing reality!

In the end, true luxury is defined by quality and refinement. Any item of luxury is a presentation of highly skilled work, which can only be borne from an endless pursuit for perfection.

I am in awe whenever I see 19th-century craftsmanship of jewellery from the Napoleonic era. As an artist in the 21st century, utilizing a centuries old craft, I am very honoured to have the ability to pass on this long lost artistry for generations to come. I hope more artists will be able to understand and continue this sophisticated delicate craft, which captures the real essence behind jewellery art. I will always admire people who continue to challenge themselves, and leave their comfort zone in order to achieve greatness. —CC

Royal BUTTERFLY

The astonishing Royal Butterfly Masterpiece perfectly embodies Cindy Chao's talent and skill, and represents the pinnacle of her creative genius. One single piece is meticulously created each year, and this particular design has been inducted into the National Museum of Natural History at the Smithsonian Institute in Washington DC, and was the first piece of jewellery to ever grace the cover of *Women's Wear Daily*, in the publication's 100-year history.

The design for the Royal Butterfly began in 2006 when Chao found striking pairs of rough-cut diamonds at the Baselworld, international jewellery show in Switzerland. "I was mesmerized by the natural patterns of the diamonds, which reminded me of the microstructure on a butterfly's wings." From childhood Chao has been drawn to butterflies—their vibrant, flourishing colours; their short lifespan; their light, delicate and graceful flight. But it was to be some time before she began designing this iconic piece of jewellery.

The catalyst came a few months later on a sultry summer day in bustling Hong Kong. "I was walking in Central, between high-rises and busy crowds, I felt harassed by the heat, the honking of car horns and pushy pedestrians. Suddenly, I saw a colourful butterfly gently float by, it stopped on a post on the street corner and for that moment I felt like I was in another world, where everything was peaceful and tranquil: the Royal Butterfly was born."

Chao and her team of master craftsmen used nearly 77 carats of gemstones to create the first piece. Made up of over 2,300 colour diamonds, inky sapphires, rubies and vivid green tsavorites, Chao incorporated 20 colour gradients to perfectly mimic the breathtakingly brilliant shades of a butterfly's wings.

"The Royal Butterfly represents a breakthrough in technique for my work. Each gemstone had to be secured by four prongs and each of the nearly 10,000 prongs had to be planted during the wax molding phase. To enhance the fire and brilliance of the rough diamonds on the butterfly's wings, we placed a layer of diamonds underneath and invented the layering setting technique for my art jewellery pieces. My creations were now not only viewable from every angle, but were actually designed from the inside out."

Each gemstone on the butterfly has to be fitted tightly against the next, which was a challenge for Chao and her team given the differences in shape and size. "The gems had to be seamlessly and smoothly set, it was up to the skilful master craftsmen to measure the precise dimensions of every stone and determine how and where to mount it, while staying true to my original design. It was as if the butterfly was coming out of its cocoon." After two years of work the metamorphosis was complete.

*"I saw a colourful butterfly gently float by;
it stopped on a post on the street corner, and for that moment
I felt like I was in another world."*

The Royal Butterfly, 2009 Masterpiece I

Winter Branch, 2009 Masterpiece VI, Four Seasons Collection

Winter ICE

"The Winter Branch Brooch is elaborate, exquisite and extensive, taking eighteen months to create. My somber mood is represented in this piece, by its crisp, cold, bold two-tone colours."

Many artists cite nature as their inspiration, but few attempt to capture the chilly, barren depths of winter in a piece of jewellery. So it is a creative designer who can find something of ethereal beauty in this sparse, pared-back season, and create a piece so eye-catchingly different, it is showcased at one of the world's leading auction houses. Christie's New York selected Cindy Chao's Winter Series from the Four Seasons Collection in 2007, propelling Chao and her jewellery into a recognizable—and established—global brand.

The Winter Branch Brooch has an icy, remote beauty. The brooch starts as several separate pieces; the knotted branches are made from overlapping collars, then encrusted with black and white diamonds. Individual mechanisms allow these limbs to be reconnected for a flawless finish. The delicate dangling foliage is represented by marquise diamonds, joined only at one or two points with the optimal angle suitable for each diamond taken into consideration, to ensure maximum brilliance. The piece is elaborate, exquisite and extensive, making the 18-month design process seem effortless.

"The significance of the Winter Branch Brooch is especially close to my heart, representing a time in my life when I faced hardships, both on a personal level and as a jewellery artist. I decided to take a risk, and break away from the dictates of conventional jewellery, instead following the true creation of artistry and pioneering new craftsmanship to realize my dream. At first those around me were unable to come to grips with my vision. My somber mood is represented in this piece, by the crisp, cold, bold two tone colors of the winter branch."

"Everybody has a dream. I still remember the days when I was studying in New York City. Every time I passed by Christie's head office at Rockefeller Center, I would stop in my tracks, stare at the grand entrance, and pray that one day my jewellery designs would outshine all others, and that my work would eventually be auctioned at Christie's. In December 2007, my dream came true. From that moment on, I was more determined than ever to create one of a kind artistry—the Art Jewel."

Interna FLAWLESS

One of the uniquely defining characteristics of Cindy Chao's breathtaking jewellery is that no matter which angle you look at a piece from, it is complete—the back, sides, and underside are as detailed and meticulously observed as the front. Vivid colours and temperaments are masterfully woven into a complex 360-degree composition, featuring layers of delicately placed jewels.

The Four Seasons Collection is one of Cindy Chao's signature lines, and perfectly highlights her singular skill as a designer and craftsman. "This ode to the seasons features a heightened state of sensitivity to nature, each art piece in the collection reveals a diversion from the traditional look of fine jewelry into a form far more emotionally engaging," says Chao. The two featured rings make dramatic use of space, vibrant shots of colour, and structured layers to represent changes in the seasons.

The sumptuous Spring Lily ring, which took twelve months to bring to life, features a natural 4.76 carat rosy conch pearl gently accented with tsavorites. Rose gold strips and white gold diamonds make up the petals, and stems of black diamonds are entwined to forge the ring's band. "Through this ring the waking life of a lily is captured as it edges from spring into a full summer bloom," says

Chao. "Each characteristic—the swaying pistils, a shot of coloration with the uncurled petals—contributes to this slow-motion transition." Effortlessly elegant, the ring has special meaning for Chao as the lily is one of her favourite flowers, symbolising purity and virtue.

Surrounding a 1.54 carat chameleon diamond—one of the rarest gems in the world—the jaw-dropping autumn Maple Leaf Ring is comprised of two layers and twelve gradients of warm yellow, champagne and brown diamonds, emulating nature's autumn palette. Also taking a year to create, the exceptional translucence of the ring is due to the placement of brilliant round diamonds, set in between the irregularly shaped, undulating rose-cut diamonds which make up the icy white layer on the leaf.

"The ring is a representation of the continuous activity during autumn, and in life. In the autumn season before the hibernation of winter, the pace of life winds down, but movement and change is still at hand," says Chao. "The selection of the chameleon diamond is a mirror reflecting the gorgeous spectrum of autumn hues."

lly

"*This ring captures the lily as it edges from spring into full summer bloom.*"

TOP RIGHT: *Spring Lily ring, 2007 Masterpiece X, Four Seasons Collection*
ABOVE: *Autumn Maple Leaf ring, 2009 Masterpiece XIII, Four Seasons Collection*

"From each angle, the ring becomes a gift anew."

Top and side views of blue sapphire ring, Ribbons Collection

Jewelled RIBBONS

It was the elegant wrapping, rather than the gift, that inspired one of Cindy Chao's most magnificent creations. Struck by how the ribbon on a present had been tied, she set about creating the fabric's intricate folds and creases in precious metals and gemstones. "This simple ritual, performed by the gift bearer, triggers a myriad of thrilling emotions; that delightful excitement the recipient feels in anticipation of what lies inside—fingers eagerly seek to unravel the intertwined ribbons."

The artist spent months tying various strands of ribbon hundreds of different ways, to fully understand the structural flow of material, before the Ribbons Collection came into being in 2009. Its stunning centerpiece is the 18.89 carat blue sapphire; the mesmerising stone—'the gift'—is gracefully wrapped in diamond-encrusted lengths of jewelled ribbon. "I tied countless ribbons during the design process, but never once did they look exactly the same," says Chao. "It speaks to the ethos of my jewellery design; all my creations are one of a kind."

Recreating soft and silky fabric in precious metals and gemstones posed huge obstacles during production. Using hard wax molding to emulate flexible cloth presented significant new challenges for the craftsmen, and this piece took a total of 18 months to evolve. Playing with the color gradients to showcase light, shadow, and silhouettes, imitating the fall and curve of the material, was an elaborate process, with each stone individually and painstakingly laid.

The design has a 360-degree composition, giving the piece fluidity of motion, just like a ribbon. White diamonds creased with blue sapphires are mounted with micro-settings under a 40x magnifier; each jewel is set so tightly against the next that even from the back, no metal can be seen to the naked eye. "Every angle of the ring becomes a fantastical life form," says Chao. "The undulating ribbons frolicking playfully around this gift represent my core inspiration for the series—a bow-tie that possesses a life of its own, enticing the bearer to unwrap it. From each angle, the ring becomes a gift anew."

Layered FANTASY

"In the process of bringing this design to life, the fan became symbolic in another way — it imbues the spirit of dedication."

It is easy to imagine this magical work of art adorning a fêted Chinese beauty's dressing table, and indeed, its creation is bound around the notion that in ancient times, every Chinese belle had her very own fan. Made up of a staggering 2,399 Forevermark diamonds weighing over 310 carats, Chao spent almost a year, day and night, making her vision an amazing reality. It is all the more remarkable a feat, considering Chao was originally told her final design was too intricate, and could not actually be realized. But with sheer determination to push boundaries, passion and pioneering craftsmanship, Chao has created a stunning masterpiece.

"As with many great designs, the problem tends to lie in the execution; creating the fragile structure of the 25cm by 45cm fan was an enormous task, but I was fortunate to work with my talented in-house team of craftsmen," says Chao. "The first stage began with wax molding, which took over a month, and I was only getting three hours of sleep a night. The sleepless nights continued for another seven months, until the piece was finally finished."

Delicate, intertwining 18k gold vines have been set with Forevermark pave diamonds in order to shape the 360-degree, three-layer coiled branches, mimicking the curves, skeletal textures and tones of tree branches and trunks. With a stroke of genius, a detachable butterfly brooch made of 18K rose, white and yellow gold and Forevermark diamonds, is set into the lower left corner of the fan. As the world's leading diamond group, with over a century's worth of expertise, De Beers and Forevermark's Precious Collection selects diamonds and jewelry designers with exceptional qualities and talent; less than 1% of the world's diamonds are eligible to become a Forevermark Diamond.

"In the process of bringing this design to life, the fan became symbolic in another way; it left me with the sense I could achieve anything I wanted. It imbues the spirit of dedication," says Chao. Displayed in Beijing's Today Art Museum and Tokyo's Mori Art Museum, the Majestic Beauty Fan has cemented Cindy Chao's unique ability to successfully blur the lines between jewellery as an accessory and jewellery as art.

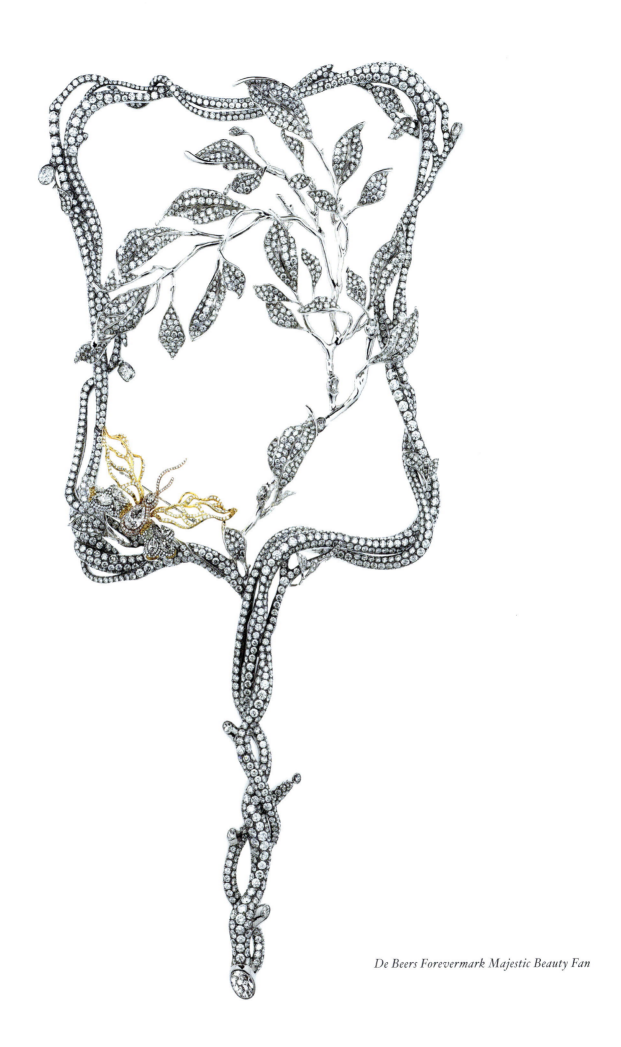

De Beers Forevermark Majestic Beauty Fan

SANDRINE CLAYTON

"To me, self-expression is an art and my designs are a depiction of all the influences in my life so far."

One of my most vivid childhood memories is my godmother's jewellery collection; from a little girl's perspective, her pieces were huge, breathtaking treasures—she loved to wear big rings. My mother was more discreet with her jewellery, but she was also an aesthete; she collected buttons, ribbons, clothes, and had one of the most incredible designer vintage collections. My favourite dress was a 1932 design with a massive onyx and diamond brooch on the hip—stunning! They were both strong, elegant, chic Frenchwomen, who instilled in me an enduring appreciation for beautiful things.

I was always encouraged to be my own person, and as a result I knew at a very young age what I liked and which styles suited me, while my peers at the time were still searching. My tastes are simple—my preferred colours are muted and I favour understatement—but I am also very eclectic in my style. I believe it is wrong to impose your ideas on others; aesthetically we are all different, and I admire people who feel happy in their own skins, people who have evolved their own personal style. 'Good taste' is difficult to define, but can be thought of, perhaps, as an aesthetic balance that might not be to everyone's exact liking, but the resulting image as a whole is flawless, and usually classic.

My designs do not follow trends and fashion, and I do not aspire to the designer item; I aspire instead to individuality. Today, luxury means uniqueness, and I have always sought to incorporate this spirit into my pieces. As a child I made rings out of cigarette packet foil or wire from champagne corks, and as I got older I created necklaces out of velvet ribbon and buttons. I had a beautiful blue 18th-century enamel and brass button that my great-aunt found in her attic and cut from a piece of clothing; I used to wear it on a beige ribbon around my neck. This was 'typical Sandrine'! When I was eighteen I melted down an Edwardian garnet and seed pearl ring my mother had given me, and made my first piece of real jewellery. I would also design a lot of pieces using semi-precious stones and pearls; even if it was as simple as taking a piece of string, knotting it and putting a pearl on the end.

Now, gems and stones are the most important things to me—I love them in their raw state, and I think stones are the most beautiful things in the world. I'm inspired by so much and I take inspiration from anything and everything—an unusual ornament in someone's home, a piece of patterned fabric, segments of pomelo on a white plate, a specific colour, the cut of a dress, my loved ones. I am very, very observant. I have experienced the culture of so many different countries—I grew up in France and Spain, went to school in England, worked at Sotheby's in Belgium, and have lived in Australia and Hong Kong—each has had an important impact on my jewellery design.

My signature style is understated yet large, unique rings, mostly for the little finger, with a fragile rawness. The gold in my designs has a lot of texture and gives the whole piece a very ancient feel. I believe my jewellery is timeless, underpinned with an ageless and distinctive spirit. The process of designing and making jewellery has always been very fluid for me, and something I've been able to do wherever I have lived. I have never wanted to work for anyone else. The best part of the job is creating and designing; I have wonderfully talented craftsmen here in Hong Kong who work with me to produce the finished pieces. I totally unwind when I'm working; for me, it is like meditation, and it is so satisfying to produce things that women love to wear, and make them look truly beautiful. —SC

SHOW

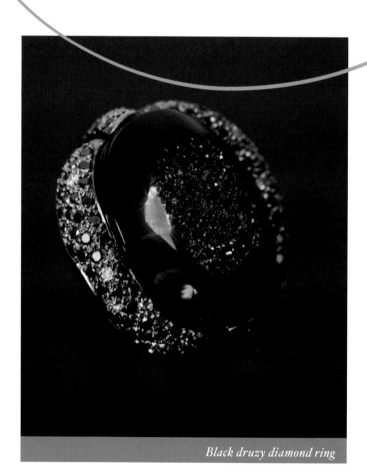

Black druzy diamond ring

"Lustrous black agate erupts out of tiny, glittering brown and black diamonds."

Sandrine Clayton's unconventional, opulent and textured pieces ooze pure, unadulterated style. Topping the glamour stakes is her Black Druzy Diamond Ring: lustrous, black agate erupts out of two carats of tiny, glittering brown and black diamonds. But the most compelling feature of the ring is the druzy shimmering on top of the agate. When water carrying dissolved silica is forced into a porous rock cavity, and there is a subsequent rapid cooling process, tiny crystals are formed on the rock's surface or in the cavity. If these clear crystals form on top of previously deposited minerals, a druzy is created.

In this piece the druzy adds a brilliantly contrasting texture, offsetting the smoothness of the agate, while enhancing the rough and earthy beauty of the diamonds. Sandrine bought the stone from a Turkish dealer at an Australian jewellery fair. She was instantly drawn to the stone but it sat untouched in her workroom for more than two years, before inspiration hit.

"I love the natural elegance of this ring. It is such a sophisticated piece of jewellery—and it is definitely a woman's ring; there is nothing immature or 'girly' about it," says Sandrine. "The design is organic and different, it has a look you don't see very often. My inspiration came from the first druzy stone I purchased a few years ago. I knew when I held it in my hand it would make a magnificent ring; I loved its rawness and uniqueness. Natural, untreated, high-quality druzies are not easy to find and it's impossible to mass produce the same quality stones—which adds to the ring's appeal. I worked with a few coloured diamonds as I wanted to reflect the crystal formation of the druzy on the agate 'host'." Colour selection was key in the making of this sumptuous piece. When selecting the diamonds, Sandrine was careful to stay away from brilliant white, which would only detract from the centre stone. Instead she carefully selected complementary shades of brown and light grey.

The setting itself also has an organic feel and for each piece she creates, Sandrine changes the texture of the gold depending on the central stone. For this ring she used a smooth and shiny black gold to further enhance the luster and depth of the druzy. "I recently made another druzy ring; the centre stone had much more texture, so I chose a rough black gold with brown tones to better complement it."

True to her signature style of understated, yet large and unique rings, Sandrine designed this piece to be worn on the little finger. "I love big rings on little fingers and I would like more women to wear rings this way; big cocktail rings." Historically, little-finger rings featured a coat of arms and were worn as a single adornment by the nobility. In more recent times, arbiters of fashion and style such as Diana Vreeland and Coco Chanel have worn distinctive rings on their little fingers: large, colourful and fantastic pieces. "I feel these rings are best worn on their own on the right hand, with nothing to detract from their beauty, but they have to be tight so they don't slip," says Sandrine.

If you want to wear the little-finger ring with other jewellery, Sandrine still prefers a simple approach. "One of the perennial questions is how much jewellery is too much: personally I don't like too many different styles or pieces worn together. If they are all the same it can work, but it's difficult to combine earrings, necklace, bracelet and rings without looking overloaded. If you want to wear a 'set', choose earrings and a bracelet, or if you're wearing a necklace, wear very small earrings. Try not to wear too many rings together; it's less impactful. A sole ring worn on your thumb or index finger can also be spectacular."

Creamy

STONES

Clayton X, Clayton's brand, is synonymous with dramatic cocktail rings; each flaunts a beautifully unique stone and setting, and all are encased in Sandrine's trademark 'beaten', textured matte gold. Using coloured gold, from black to white and every shade in-between, including pink, lends each piece a distinctive edge. "I look at the piece as a whole, it has to be a *marriage*; by changing the gold it is possible to create a totally different look. I vary it depending on the stone; moonstones look fabulous with white diamonds, black with grey is beautiful, black with white is funky, and pink diamonds on rose gold look amazing!" says Sandrine.

Manipulating the colour of the gold brings out the character of each individual stone, especially those that vary greatly in hue and texture, like jade. Sandrine uses a variety of rare and beautiful stones that are not commonly seen, such as old jade, old turquoise, tanzanite, jasper, prehnite, and chyrophrase, and combines them with diamonds to create individual and bold designs.

One of Sandrine's most impactful pieces is her glittering 31-carat old jade ring, set in 18 carats of matte grey gold, and surrounded by 1.55 carats of fancy diamonds. The creamy smoothness of the flecked-orange central stone contrasts with the irregular, knobbly texture of the pavé diamonds, and is perfectly offset by the textured grey gold.

The white jade and bezel-set diamond ring is a smaller piece, designed especially for the little finger. Set in 18-carat yellow textured matte gold, the central jade stone is one of three delicately coloured pale, creamy green buttons that Sandrine found at a local dealer in Shanghai. "I thought about making a bracelet, which would have been the logical route, but in the end I chose to create a ring. I didn't want a hole in the middle of the jade, so I filled it with a diamond to give the piece an edge. It's such a versatile ring, it would look equally fabulous with a white silk sundress, or with black, or dressed down with jeans."

In a darker hue of green, shot through with brown veins, the carved jade ring featuring a feathered scribe is also set in 18 carat yellow textured matte gold. The jade was originally part of a belt, and is double-sided; the reverse shows a carved scroll. "Again, most would have chosen to feature the scroll, but I loved the scribe; the jade is from the period in Chinese history where the literati, the intelligentsia were vastly influential."

Another carved jade ring features an intricate dragon in relief on brown jade, which Sandrine also sourced from China. "I love the fact I live in Asia and can use jade, a stone that is so important to Chinese culture; for me it's like an homage. I am subconsciously influenced by the things I see around me, so Asian stones and an Asian

> *"I look at the piece as a whole — it has to be a marriage. By changing the gold, it is possible to create a totally different look."*

influence necessarily pervade aspects of my jewellery." One of her jade rings (not shown) has a smooth, aged, nut-brown surface, clocking in at a staggering 52 carats. It is beautifully complemented by the 18-carat yellow textured matte gold surrounding the stone.

Her 28.46-carat moonstone ring has a silky luster, reminiscent of a large black pearl. Sandrine has again chosen to show off the smooth beauty of the central stone with a surrounding cluster of tiny coloured diamonds (1.75 carats) and a matte grey-gold setting, emphasizing the contrast between rough and smooth.

"If you're going to buy a ring, know what you like," says Sandrine. "Have an image in your head; if you don't love it, don't even bother thinking about how you could change it — keep searching for the right one!" She will also custom-make rings for clients, combining their existing stones and her own design philosophy. "My job is to guide my clients and help them choose something that will remain a classic for their personality and lifestyle. The ultimate aim is for the client to have a piece of jewellery they love wearing, and would pass on to their children."

FROM TOP: *White jade ring, carved jade rings, moonstone and diamond ring, aged jade and diamond ring*

*Wood beaded necklace
and gold prayer beads*

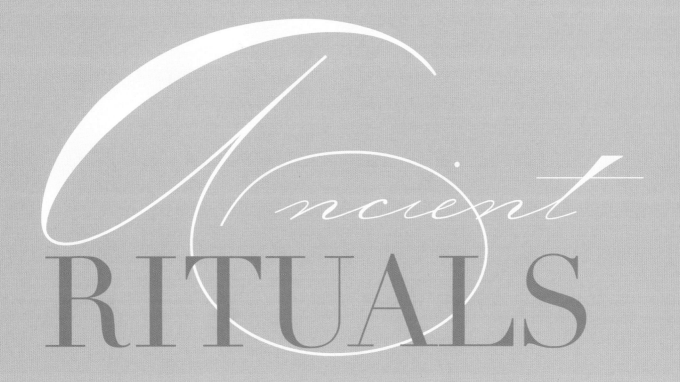

RITUALS

Ancient

"Each strand is infused with decades of heady incense smoke."

Sandrine's boxwood beaded necklace tells an ancient story: one of monks, prayer beads and mystic chanting. She sources the century-old strands of prayer beads in antique shops both in Hong Kong and China; the older pieces are becoming increasingly difficult to find. Each strand is infused with decades of heady incense smoke, which combines with the boxwood to give an aromatic and soothing scent that lingers on the fingers. "I love the fact they look so old and worn, and I love the colour; wood takes such a long time to age," says Sandrine.

"Prayer beads originate from after the Crusades—it's where the rosary comes from—and they feature in so many religions, from Islam to Buddhism. All these religions have a form of chanting where you move from one bead to the next. If you string the prayer beads with small gold beads, as I have, it's very simple, but the effect is beautiful. I have also placed a simple piece of jade on the necklace to give it added interest." All of Sandrine's beads are hand-strung by a 75-year-old woman in Hong Kong: "She's the best beader on the planet, even though her hands are knarled with arthritis."

Individually knotted around each vermeil bead, a cappuccino-coloured silk thread offsets the brilliant yellow hue of the vivid gold vermeil necklace. The design comes in two lengths (45 or 61 inches), and can be worn together or separately. Each strand can be looped around the neck to create the effect of choker and necklace together; Sandrine's signature look. "I like the very long length, the length that hangs just below your belly button. A choker around the neck is always sophisticated; it makes the neck look longer and more elegant. But I made both a long and a mid-length because I wanted to give the wearer options; it makes the necklaces very versatile." The beads are classically Indian in design, and typically used to decorate clothing; no one else has used them in isolation, or strung them quite like Sandrine. Vermeil is a French word describing sterling silver that has been electroplated with at least 100 millionths of an inch of carat gold.

Unadulterated GLAMOUR

Sandrine's trademark style is stamped all over this extraordinary 9.8-carat diamond ring, despite the fact the design and setting are quite different to those of her other pieces. It is rare to find a large diamond in such a massive setting that still retains a sense of lightness and elegance, yet can be comfortably worn every day. The Indian diamond is surrounded by 3.6 carats of cognac, champagne and white tiny diamonds which fold in and around the central stone to give it sparkle, helping lift and brighten the piece; the 18-carat yellow textured matte gold is very pale, perfectly complementing the colour of the stones. "I love India, its culture and its jewellery; look at the incredible pieces the Indian maharajahs used to wear. And of course, most stones come from India," says Sandrine.

Following traditional Indian craftsmanship, the central stone is held in place by a yellow gold casing which wraps around the back of the stone. The inside of the casing is platinum and white gold, creating a mirrored effect for the large diamond, accenting its beauty and colour. Sandrine has ingeniously hidden the casing by covering it with her signature lattice-work gold, making the back a work of art in itself. "I want all my jewellery to look lovely from the back; I'm a perfectionist. I was originally inspired by the Byzantine and Egyptian collections at the British Museum in London; I remember seeing a piece that belonged to

a Damascan or Syrian governor of the Roman Empire, it was an engraved cornelian stone ring. My jewellery has a very Roman feel, I want each design to look as if it has come out of the earth, out of an ancient tomb."

Sandrine designed the piece for herself, but plans to use the basic design to create similar rings with different stones, including sapphires and seed pearls. "The setting is playful and has the same roundness as the stone; it's considered a very French setting because of its size. In France women are comfortable wearing rings this big every day! Of course, you wouldn't wear any other jewellery with this piece, perhaps only a pair of small earrings and a watch. I didn't want a typical solitaire, I wanted a deep-set diamond with stones surrounding it, and I wanted to convey a sense of rawness. But the edging is still pretty, and the diamond is a surprise!"

"When I made the mould I changed it three times to get it exactly right, although I did a number of preliminary drawings. I have several diamond dealers and I gave them a prescriptive brief—the first thing I said was that I wasn't interested in VV1, I'm simply looking for a beautiful, original stone. The stone has a crack deep inside, and I like the fact it has character. The whole aesthetic is that you are buying a work of art, and you either like it or you don't. But to me, every aspect of this ring is beautiful."

"My jewellery has a very Roman feel. I want each design to look as if it has come out of the earth, out of an ancient tomb."

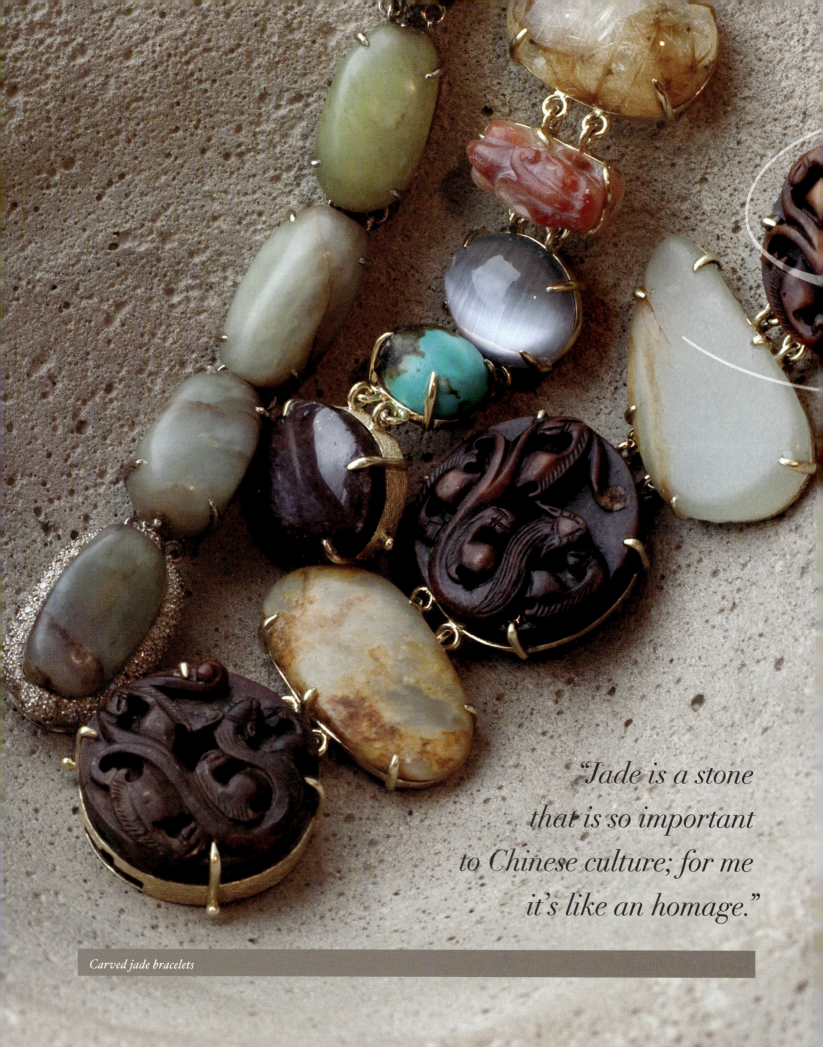

"Jade is a stone
that is so important
to Chinese culture; for me
it's like an homage."

Carved jade bracelets

Timeless BEAUTY

Few jewellers embrace organic design as successfully as Sandrine Clayton; each stone from her tactile, satisfyingly chunky bracelets could have been picked up on a beach or dug from deep in the earth; each unique combination of stones flows organically and logically. "In line with the general trend towards all things natural, these bracelets have a truly organic feel," says Sandrine. "But I have also definitely been influenced by the sophistication and fluidity of modern day Hong Kong, and this has given the pieces an unusual and interesting twist."

Three carved phoenixes and a cockerel characterize Sandrine's unusual jade bracelet; six pieces of relatively heavy jade have been set into delicate 18-carat gold links to give the bracelet a remarkably light and airy feel. Sandrine found the jade with the carved cockerel several years before coming across the other pieces of old jade, and knew immediately they would make a stunning bracelet. "I carried the carved cockerel with me all the time, hunting for pieces of jade to complement it. When you first see the bracelet, it looks a little bohemian, but a few of my clients have tried the piece on, and it suits everyone; it's very warm. At a jewellery exhibition in Hong Kong one Chinese lady spent three days coming back and repeatedly looking at it. In the end she told me it was the first time she had seen a successful fusion of her culture with Western culture, that was pleasing to the eye. That was a huge compliment to me!"

One of the first pieces of jewellery Sandrine ever made was a multi-gem bracelet, and combining stones of different textures and hues remains one of her passions. Reminiscent of boiled sweets, the multi-gem bracelet is composed of old turquoise, carved jade, garnet, wispy phantom quartz, citrine and luscious star ruby, sourced over the years from China and India. "It's a very happy piece," says Sandrine. "I love the colours; they are fun, yet sophisticated. In fact, this was a seminal piece for me—the carved clasp started my hallmark carved back, which is on all my jewellery."

The third bracelet, in jade, is the last word in elegance. Composed of five milky green, old jade pieces, the 1.01 carat of fancy diamonds on the 18-carat grey-gold clasp add a subtle hint of glamour. "I love the grey gold with the earthy colour of the old jade," says Sandrine. "It's a symphony of East and West, the oriental jade against the European design of the clasp. I have always been very eclectic in my style, but my latest collection is slightly different from earlier ones, I feel it is more grown up. It is, however, still true to my design ethos: timeless, unique, quality, without following trends or fashion. Now I want people to see the more sophisticated side of *Clayton X*."

JEAN-FRANÇOIS FICHOT

"It is not about the clarity of a stone or the rarity of a metal; it's about beauty and meaning. It is about finding an exotic, natural stone and creating a one-off piece that is precious, yet intoxicatingly flamboyant."

Arriving in Bali in 1978, I fell in love with the people, the culture and the beauty of the place. The mysticism and spiritual energy of Asia has always been in my blood; my heart and soul belong to the ancient shrines, rainforests and vibrant people of the Far East. I had traveled from my home in France to India in the 70s, and was completely mesmerized by its rich history and culture. As a child I pored over pictures of the great maharajahs, laden in their exquisite jewels, and it was these ancient stories and colourful people that formed the inspiration for much of my early work, and remain an integral part of my design ethos. But it was not until I reached the white shores and verdant jungles of Bali, that I found my true spiritual home. This island constantly inspires me to create my most ambitious work.

Bali is an incredibly special place; there is an energy, an enchantment which casts its spell over all artisans who call it home. The people are gentle and warm; the local craftsmen hugely gifted. When I design my jewellery and objets d'art, they inherently understand how to realize my vision. The lush, tropical vegetation, which covers most of the island, is a huge influence, and forms the backdrop to much of my work. Indeed, my second greatest obsession is gardening; my father was a talented gardener, and I have inherited his green thumb. When I travel I collect cuttings from tropical corners of the globe, so my private garden in Ubud is a botanical paradise, and I think of it as my other work of art.

I am also a collector of unusual, natural materials; I scour the globe in search of the most alluring and unique stones, woods and metals. Wandering the backstreets of Cochin in India, I might find stunning antiques; in Cuba old French perfume bottles; in Hong Kong a vivid green and pink tricolour watermelon tourmaline; or from a Brazilian dealer in Bangkok, perfect emerald crystals. My challenge is to combine old and new materials, the beliefs and cultures of East and West, the precious with the quirky, to create something sublime, fantastical and very different. Transcending the ordinary is my passion.

I am never exactly sure what I am going to do with the pieces. I am instinctively attracted to them, and my talent is to combine them. So antique Roman glass bowls I found from Afghanistan take on a completely different character when delicately edged in vine-like, 22-carat yellow gold. A carved green aventurine statue of Ganesh, Indian God of Wisdom, truly becomes one of a kind when embellished with raw diamonds, Burmese lavender jade, Chinese jade, sterling silver and 18-carat gold. These objects eclipse their original function to become something completely bewitching.

Hindu and Buddhist tales and beliefs are constant themes in my work, as are the ancient cultures of Mesopotamia, Rome and Egypt. I love to include primitive elements such as excavated glass, precious beads and beaten gold and silver in my designs. Of course, I like all gems, but I do prefer the shape of the cabochon, so smooth and round. They have an old fashioned and more natural feel, which instinctively appeals to me. I would always choose a stone in its organic state that has not been heated, still as nature intended; there is a special energy behind them. —JFF

Queen of the Sea pearl and emerald ring, Afghani spinel cabochon ring, Balinese crystal and ruby earrings

FLAMBOYANCE

Fichot's first introduction to the island of Bali was actually in New York. "I went to a concert in Carnegie Hall and saw my first Balinese dance, and felt an immediate connection with the culture. The elaborate costumes, exotic dancing, decorative temples, tropical plants, mystical rituals—Bali has an aesthetic beauty to which I am instinctively drawn. It's the sort of place where you can create your very own paradise."

These ornate ruby and crystal earrings are a modern take on the traditional 'Subang' which Balinese women have always worn. "When I arrived in the 1970s all the women wore earrings like this; they had huge holes in their ears! It was seen as a sign of beauty and spirituality to have long, hanging ear-lobes, just as Buddha did." Traditionally the earrings were one single piece, but Fichot has brought them into the 21st century with a simple screw mechanism using gold wire hidden inside. The teardrop rubies are set into Balinese gold, atop engraved icy crystal; the coolness of the crystal is offset by the rich warmth of the 22-carat Balinese gold. "My favourite material is crystal; it is both beautiful and powerful. It is like petrified water."

The luscious raspberry-coloured cabochon ring is an Afghani spinel, from the tourmaline family. "People mistakenly think this stone is a ruby because of its colour, but it's far softer than a ruby, and a completely different composition." Like several of Fichot's pieces, the velvety ring is reminiscent of a flower bud, with a setting of beaten 22-carat gold that has been carved to represent curling petals and leaves. This is wonderfully contrasted against the textured silver of the band, which has been hammered to give a wood-like effect. The result is a ring that speaks of whispering grass, perfumed scent and sun dappled blooms. "People like the idea of fantasy; they see my garden and the way I live, and they understand there is something magical about it."

One of Fichot's most stunning creations is his pearl and emerald ring, Queen of the Sea. It is the mixture of materials—the gleaming baroque pearl with the jagged gold, textured silver and watery green emeralds—that makes it a stand out piece. "The natural shape of the pearl is like a talisman, it has a special meaning. I never know exactly what I am going to design, but I trust my instincts, and when the feeling is there I just let it flow." The clever combination of gold and silver reflects the shape of the pearl, and the precise placement of two teardrop emeralds evoke the green depths of the sea. In India, there is a special name for the mix of silver and gold: Ganga and Yamuna, India's two holy rivers which converge together. Fichot also likens it to the moon merging with the sun.

Nature's TREASURE

Fichot believes that to keep the lustre of pearls alive, they must be worn. "If you put pearls in a safe for a few years, they will die. They come to life, and look particularly alluring on a woman's bare skin, rather than worn on top of clothes. There is nothing more feminine; after all, it is said pearls are the tears of a goddess! They need to be used and loved, and they will always make you feel beautiful, no matter where or when you choose to wear them."

The baroque pearls Fichot has chosen to make this ethereal and delicate necklace are a mixture of warm gold and icy silver that has nevertheless been cleverly blended to appear seamless in design. They are Indonesian in origin, from Maluku, one of the only two places in the world (the Philippines is the other), where these uniquely coloured pearls can be found. "It is getting more and more difficult to find pearls of this caliber, which is frustrating as they are so very special, and so gratifying to work with."

In his inimitable way, Jean-François Fichot has taken something of great natural beauty and subtly enhanced it, adding touches of genius. Twenty-two and 18 carat gold has been drilled through the centre of each pearl and a delicate detail added to the top and bottom, making each look like a flower bud, picked from his own garden. "The pearls look like blossoms or berries from a tree, and I have made the links with twisted gold wire, to emulate vines." This garden-inspired necklace is all the more delightful, considering its raw materials are sourced from the ocean.

While Fichot's particular love is for rings, it was necklaces that started his career as a designer; necklaces he began selling on the soft white sands of Bali's beaches, not long after his arrival on the island. "I began by making necklaces for myself, and then my friends started asking me to make them pieces. It was a natural progression, I became a jeweller almost by mistake."

OPPOSITE: *Baroque pearl necklace*

"It is said that pearls are the tears of a goddess."

Tourmaline and ruby Naga pendant

COILS

Sinuous

> *" I am hugely influenced by India's ancient culture and rituals. The allure of this piece is the goddess' face — beautifully spiritual."*

The serene figure, rising majestically out of the winding coils of a cobra in this striking pendant is Naga Kanya, the Snake Goddess. The worship of snakes may seem incongruous to many Western civilisations, but Fichot points out it is an ancient Hindu practice that dates back centuries. "The custom of snake-worship is said to have come from the Naga clan, a progressive tribe who lived in ancient India. Naga Kanya was a princess, and the first female in her clan to attain Buddha-hood. Although I shy away from gaudy Indian style, a lot of the jewellery just blows my mind. And of course, I am hugely influenced by India's ancient culture and rituals. For me, the allure of this piece is the goddess' face, she is so beautifully spiritual."

The intricately carved tourmaline from Afghanistan is set in relief, as if the Goddess is reaching out of the pendant; the stone on her forehead is a ruby, as is the exquisite, larger kidney-shaped stone that sits beneath her. This cabochon ruby comes from Tajikistan, north of Afghanistan, and was brought to Fichot by his extensive network of dealers. Over the years, Fichot has built

significant relationships with gem dealers from every corner of the globe, who consistently offer him the most unusual and precious stones: "I have contacts from South America to Thailand, from Afghanistan to Hong Kong; I have a personal connection with each of these dealers, and so they understand what I am looking for."

The necklace is given a dazzling extra dimension with the addition of five smoky rose-cut diamonds. These have been gently pressed into 22-carat yellow gold that appears to ooze from the base of the piece, as if melting. The flat gold then transforms into curving tendrils that snake their way around the precious stones, echoing the carved coils of the tourmaline cobra. "I am particularly drawn to the rough cut diamonds of Borneo; to me they are alive, as if just picked from the bed of a river. I'm not looking for clarity; I'm looking for beauty and meaning." With its rich colours, detailed carving and extravagant finish, the necklace is reminiscent of the legendary pieces made by Cartier (who Fichot says is one of his influences) for the great maharajahs in the early 1900s.

Raw EDGES

"The pearl is gently cradled in the golden leaves of a lotus blossom. Sinuous curlicues gently wind their way towards the tourmaline."

It is easy to imagine this ravishing pendant adorning the neck of a Hollywood movie star sashaying down the red carpet. Not only is it breathtakingly lovely, it is an entirely unique one-off creation that speaks to the character of its owner. Indeed, Jean-François Fichot's designs have a devoted following amongst celebrities such as Elle McPherson, Jerry Hall, John Galliano, Sting and Trudie Styler, David Bowie and Iman, Kenzo and Diane Von Furstenberg. Even style guru and famous arbiter of taste, Andy Warhol, has acquired pieces made by Fichot. This gifted jeweller's global success is all the more laudable, considering his formal training is actually in interior design.

"Everyone has a purpose in life, and designing jewellery and objets d'art is mine. I came to Bali and fell in love; here you can let go, let creativity come to you. And I live in a part of the world where it's easy to create exquisite things."

The rich, lustrous golden pearl was found by Fichot in Bali: the incredible natural colour of these pearls can only be found in Indonesia and the Philippines. "They are the most valuable of all pearls; the colour, the luminescence, is so golden. It seems to be almost alive." The shade of the pearl perfectly offsets the 22-carat gold setting, which has been painstakingly carved to represent Fichot's garden. The pearl is gently cradled in the golden leaves of a lotus blossom, as sinuous curlicues gently wind their way towards the tourmaline. The gold that lies against the deep-green stone has been cunningly crafted to mimic a wave sucking back from the shore; the grooves echo the leaves of the lotus blossom, bringing this extraordinary piece together.

"The natural tourmaline is from Brazil; the stone has not been touched, this is exactly the way it was found in the ground. It's like something you could find in a pirate's treasure chest; it could be from an antique collection but it still has such a modern feel." The stone certainly has a mesmerizing glow, and could easily be imagined as phosphorus in dark water, a jagged icicle or a light sabre! Fichot has contrasted the flatness of the stone with the bulbous curve of the pearl, creating a phenomenal piece imbued with his distinctive talent and flair.

Baroque pearl and tourmaline pendant

LUSH Lines

For years, Jean-François Fichot owned a book he kept returning to, full of pictures of elaborate 16th and 17th-century Indian carvings. So when he found the imperial topaz stone from a Brazilian dealer in Hong Kong, he knew its smooth contours would provide a perfect backdrop against which to bring these carvings dramatically back to life, in the shape of a stunning ring. "I fell in love with this stone, which so reminded me of amber, and I had it carved in Bali, with the ancient Garden Goddess. I then encased it in decorative gold leaves and flowers. This ring combines two of my greatest interests, gardening and India. I adore the India of the past and all its traditions, the beautiful Portuguese buildings in Cochin, the noise, the colour and the bustle—and it pleases me to feel I am keeping this amazing history alive. The carving on this ring is something you'll never see again, it's truly one of a kind."

But the stimulus behind the breathtaking carvings that adorn much of Fichot's jewellery are not limited to Asia; his tourmaline ring, depicting the astrological sign of Aries—Jean-François's own birthsign—is a nod towards the world of astronomy and the stars. "This ring symbolizes the sun. In old times gold was believed to be a symbol of the sun and prosperity, so I chose to embellish the ram's head and the diamond-sun with 22-carat gold."

Fichot's talented craftsmen have delicately carved the ram and behind his body, the rays of the sun. The entire ring is wrapped in a band of carved gold, which curves sinuously around the stone. Fichot has chosen silver for the base of the ring, perfectly complementing the cloudy diamond at the centre of the sun. "While this diamond from Borneo might not be good enough to use on its own, it works perfectly as part of this symbolic ring."

The extraordinary watermelon Paraiba tourmaline is the first thing one notices about the last ring, until the eye is drawn to the intricate carvings of the 22-carat gold setting. The inspiration, of course, comes from Fichot's own verdant garden. Vines, leaves, roots and flowers twist and wind around one another to gently hold the stone, complementing rather than detracting from its spectacular beauty. "This stone is so very dramatic, with the dark tourmaline green-blue colour at one end, and the deep pink at the other. It is particularly special to me because I only bought one piece; now it would be impossible to replicate, as the stones are mined in Pairaba, a tiny state in Brazil, and are very difficult to find. It is so appealing because, alongside its vivid flamboyance, it has a natural, earthy feel."

Imperial topaz ring

"*Gardens are my inspiration.*"

Aries tourmaline ring

Watermelon Paraiba tourmaline ring

WYNN
WYNN
ONG

*"I have been drawn to the unique,
and the quirky, my entire life.
I believe jewellery should be one of
a kind and crafted by hand."*

My head is filled with ideas; I am inspired by everything I see, touch, and smell. I need only a spark … some magic … a seed of a wondrous story. It could be as simple as visiting our beach house which sits on the lip of an idyllic cove, the breeze full of the scent of blooming forest trees; or walking in Paris and turning the corner of a small street to have an enchanting vignette revealed to me. Inspiration can even come from fragmentary dreams, but in order to make them tangible, consideration and research must play their parts. Fleeting thoughts must be toiled upon so they can be made flesh. Each of my pieces has personal significance; all are bound by my passion for craft and the time I spend creating each one.

I have never stuck to the rules. I am equally capable of mixing a small piece of driftwood with cognac diamonds, rose gold, and horn, as I am of mixing sea glass from a tumbled 7-Up bottle with a grouping of rare Afghan emeralds and pink sapphires. The design has to feel right to me: the proportions, colour, balance, and emotions it conveys, must be exact. I seem to have been constructing and deconstructing things my entire life. When I am conceptualizing a collection I work like a whirling dervish. My mind and hands sort and pile, mix and match, and I am forever pulling out trays of this and that—gems, leather, wood, horn, polished, tumbled, and faceted citrine, turquoise, labradorite, ametrine, tourmalines, amethyst, smoky quartz, and other semi-precious stones.

My frame of mind when I'm designing and making the piece is very different; I take my time. I like to work uninterrupted and often in solitude, accompanied only by music. People ask why I concentrate on things that may not necessarily be seen. Why do I spend weeks researching the texture of bark, or the way an insect's legs fold? It may not be noticed by someone else, but I would know, and for me that is reason enough.

I took workshops on goldsmithing and metalworking before setting up my Manila studio. I already had a good grasp of what went into creating a piece from conception to finish, but I wanted to be able to do everything myself. Ignorance is bliss in some ways; without formal training, I chase a certain look I have in mind, I am not constrained by what is supposedly possible.

I started by playing with my mother's collection of semi-precious beads, mixing them with gold, silver, and assorted copper wire. I learned to weave rings, brooches, and cuffs, by trial and error. Everything is easier in theory than reality, but I am tenacious, and I enjoy challenges. I believe in the process of learning by doing.

My formal life as a designer began at the urging of a longtime friend, Michael Salientes, one of Manila's most respected stylists. We met for lunch in 2001 and he noticed my gem and crystal-encrusted gold wire cuff. He grabbed my arm and asked where I got it. When I laughingly told him I made it while sitting on my bed during a bout of insomnia, he told me to immediately approach the famous Italian accessories store Corso Como, because he had never seen anything like it.

I write. I love to cook, to build and do interiors. I currently chair the board of one of the largest non-profit volunteer foundations in the Philippines—Hands On Manila; I've been involved since its start. I think we owe it to ourselves to do as many things as we can in life.

I would like to think of my jewellery as art. I hope my creations will not only stand the test of time, but will also be appreciated as celebrations of craftsmanship and painstaking attention to the smallest details; each one tries to successfully marry form and function. The term 'designer' is fluid. It could apply to everyone and anyone. We all create things in different ways. —WWO

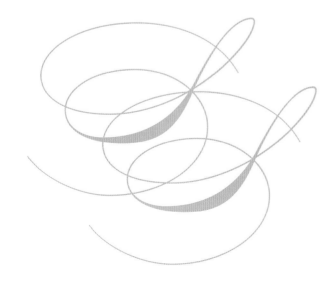

SIN
SIN

"Follow the path that is laid in front of you, let everything simply evolve. Being a spontaneous, free spirit is one of the ways to truly express your creativity."

I was raised in a Taoist temple in Hong Kong's Diamond Hill, where my grandfather rented two wings of the old building from the resident monks. Each morning the aroma of incense and the sound of singing woke me. There were young women making bamboo offerings to feed hungry ghosts, and worshippers climbing the temple stairs to bring mangoes, dragonfruit, lychees and flowers for festivals. Every afternoon I walked back from school amongst colourful red and yellow gardens, green fields filled with leafy vegetables and pungent pig farms. There was life and colour at every turn.

As a child, I learnt to be a keen observer of both rural and city life. For a treat, my grandfather would take me to Central to see the bustling city markets, and visit his office. My grandmother would pick me up from school and take me to the opera, a shared passion that is still very much alive today! We'd travel by ferry and tram, as there was no MTR or subway back then. In my family I was famous for making and doing things, designing clothes, choreographing dances, practicing calligraphy, sketching, and singing opera.

Today, my expression of personal creativity is about championing hand-picked artists and selecting special works of art to hang on the Sin Sin Atelier gallery walls; sourcing unusual fabrics and textiles from which to sculpt the clothing line; designing ornamental handbags, or an elegant and sophisticated line of jewellery. Jewellery is simply another way to accessorise and express yourself, so it's all about the individual stones you pick; it's important you feel drawn to a particular stone. It must speak to you. It's the same with a painting. It is a taste or reflection of you, your life, your choices. After all, jewellery is adornment, and adornment is art. I began making jewellery simply for myself, but so many friends asked for pieces, I have ended up making signature collections.

I opened my Atelier and fine art gallery in Hong Kong in 1998. It is a platform for an artistic community, an opportunity for well-known and some lesser-known Asian artists to showcase their work in a world city. Quite a few of my artists buy land with the money they make from selling their paintings in Hong Kong and build their own, local galleries.

History is history, now is now. You cannot predict the future, so be good today, and appreciate what you have! —SS

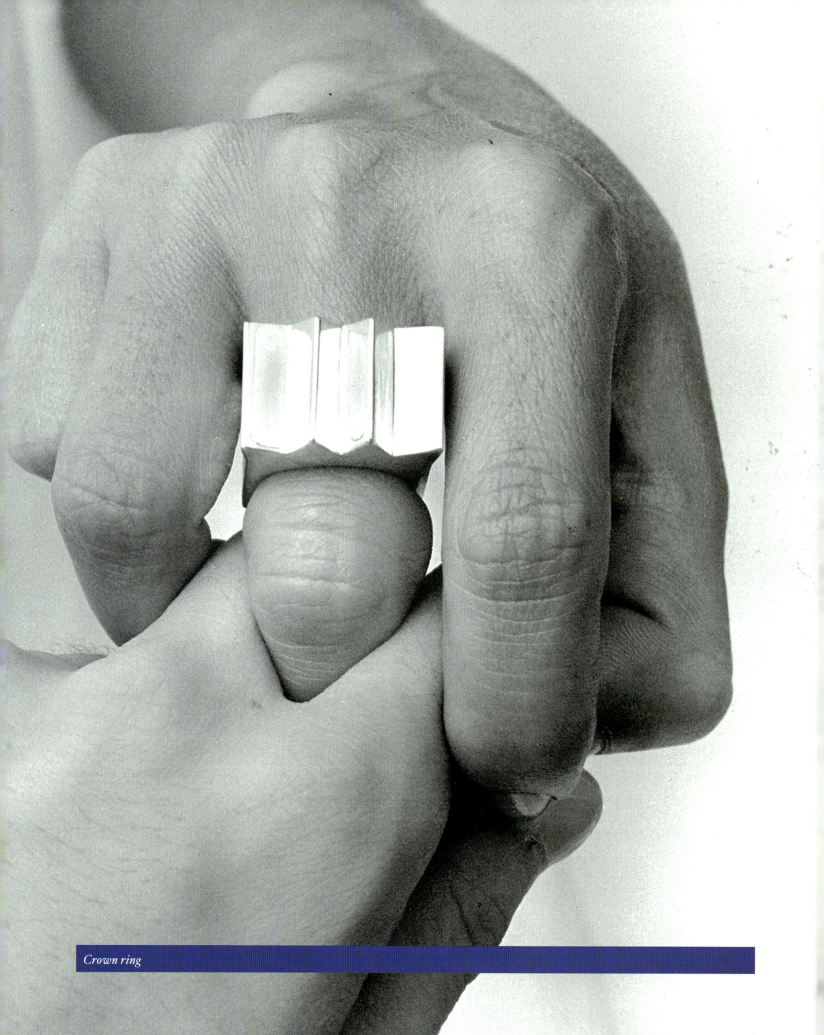

Crown ring

BOLD *Lines*

"Space is something we miss in Hong Kong. Whatever materials I use to build a house or make jewellery — whether wood or stone — I always see the lines."

Tucked away on a southerly corner of the fragrant isle of Bali, surrounded by lush rice paddies, is a peaceful home that effortlessly blends into the exotic countryside. Brainchild of Sin Sin and star architect Gianni Francione, the low sloping roofs, lustrous teak structures, quiet open spaces and simple lines of Villa SinSin formed the inspiration for the designer's strikingly pared-back range of silver jewellery.

"While building my home in Bali, I was motivated to create an architectural, sculptural line of jewellery. Both have a very simple aesthetic, and if you were to see my house from the air, you would think it was a sculpture! Whatever the materials used, when building a house or making jewellery, wood or stone, I always see the lines. There is so much open space — there are no walls except around the bedroom — and space is something we miss in Hong Kong. True minimalism is too cold for me, so I thought very carefully about the colours and materials used, trying to blend the structure as much as possible into the natural surroundings. It's very sculptural, the way the tiles are laid, the reflections in the water ... the house is very calm."

The jewellery collection is full of unexpected pairings of curves and sharp lines. Horizontals and diagonals complement smooth domed surfaces in a sophisticated and very modern take on jewellery design. One silver ring clasps a heart-shaped black, glossy stone, which has a natural, subtle indentation in its centre. "These stones are naturally formed this way, it's a little like the dimple on a peach," says Sin Sin. Another bold piece is structured like a turret on a castle, and yet another looks like the gear on a bike or a piece of machinery. One of the star pieces in the collection is the chunky crown-shaped ring, which sits snugly on the middle finger of the hand. Despite its weight, it is surprisingly comfortable.

Indigenous
SHAPES

"I wanted to incorporate my love of nature into the piece. Flowers, fruit and leaves have always been an important part of my story."

Part of Sin Sin's aesthetic is her total disregard for the dollar value of precious stones and materials; she would as soon design with quartz as with pure white diamonds. For Sin Sin, it is all about creating something beautiful that has meaning, and expresses the true self.

With her sculptural silver necklace, one of her earliest designs, it is completely up to the wearer to decide how best to put on the piece; to show either the glossy side of the sterling-silver starfruit-shaped pieces, or the contrast of the matte side. Held delicately together by silver chains running down either side, the articulated necklace falls fluidly around the neck, no matter how you decide to wear it. The silver has been oxidized on the reverse side to create a blackened hue, which gives the piece an almost ancient and tribal feel.

"At the time I designed this, I was still very influenced by all things sculptural, but I wanted to incorporate my love of plants and nature into the piece. I could see the big leaves in my garden, the natural beauty around me. The end result is something that could be interpreted in many different ways. Flowers, fruit and leaves have always been an important part of my story. The earth is nature."

Over the past two decades Sin Sin's jewellery has evolved, but still reflects her chaotic passion to create, and her simple, elegant, sculptural forms. "I don't remember the first pieces I designed, they were so spontaneous. I just enjoy the process of creating. I live in the present, so if you ask me what I'll be doing in five years time, I couldn't tell you!"

Double-textured silver necklace

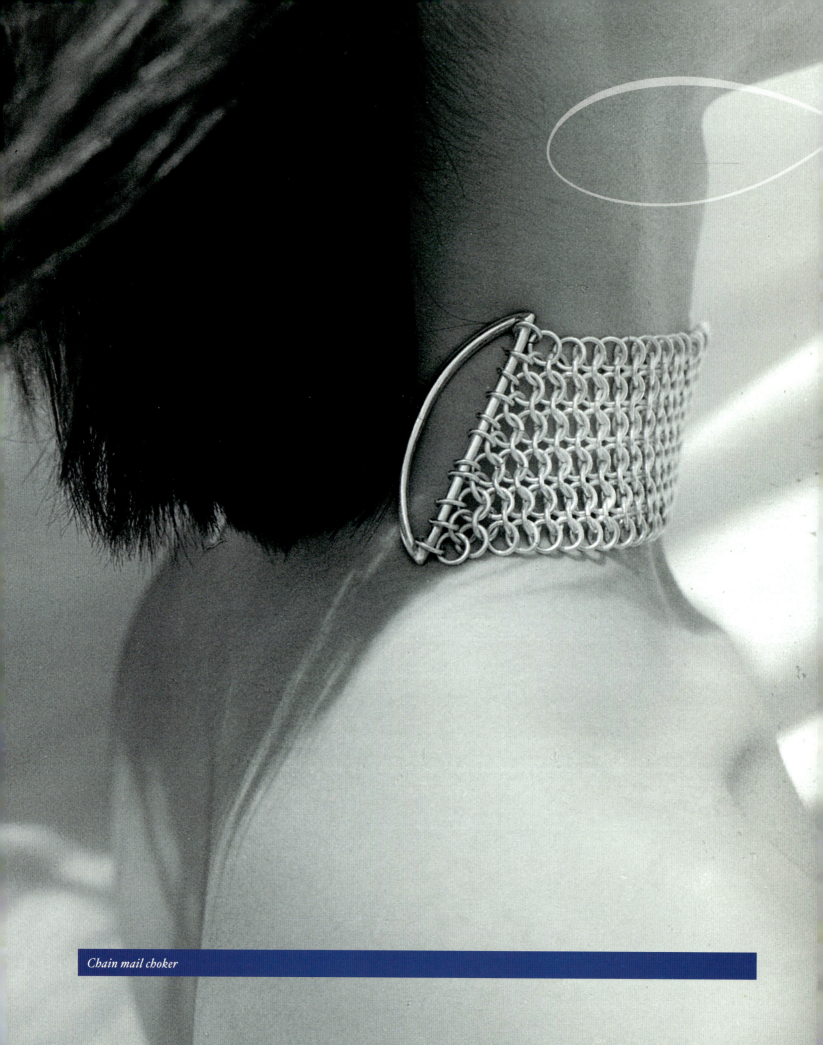

Chain mail choker

"It is shaped so sensuously it molds to your skin, almost like armour."

There is a special quality about something that has been handmade. Perhaps, it is the soul of the artisan contained within the object, the small imperfections that make it beautiful, or the fact that it is uniquely yours, and yours alone. Some years ago Sin Sin discovered a village artist who was famous for making surprisingly delicate items out of finely linked chain mail, and a partnership was born. Together, they created a dramatic and regal choker that stays beautifully true to her pared-back design ethos.

"It is shaped so sensuously it molds to your skin, almost like armour. It's also very architectural. The choker can be adjusted at the back, and there is a long chain that hangs down between the shoulder blades. These pieces entail a lot of work; the craftsman puts each link together by hand, and it takes days and days". At either end of the necklace is a semi-circular-shaped silver ring shaped rather like a horse-bit. It has been gently molded into a curve to lay against the neck.

Part of the choker's appeal is its versatility. It can be worn by almost anyone, and thanks to the clever design of the chain at the back of the necklace, it can be adjusted to any length. When Sin Sin was looking to photograph the piece, she chose a young, skinny boy who was working with the hairdresser on the shoot to model the piece. The designer did all the styling and art direction herself, and the end result is stunning. "I never care about pretty faces. I care about character, which is more important than beauty. It is you who defines what you are wearing, and not the designer."

STRONG
Statements

"You can wear two or three bracelets together.
They are heavy, solid, but feel great on your arm."

A large part of Sin Sin's prodigious inspiration is drawn from her extensive travels. Although Hong Kong is her base, she moves from place to place, exploring new cultures and hidden destinations. So no one was more surprised than Sin Sin, when she found herself returning time and time again to Bali. "Bali has a strong energy, and my first visit was an enlightening experience. There is an inherent support for creativity in Bali, and that is why I felt such an affinity to the island."

Much of Sin Sin's jewellery is influenced by Indonesia, and Bali in particular; the collection is crafted by a group of traditional Balinese silversmiths. Her works are rooted in Oriental values that are often mixed with influences from the West. Her sterling silver square ring, she says, reminds her of a Pandora's Box!

"The silversmith who worked on this design is an old, skinny guy with long hair, and he spends much of his day sitting in an old wooden chair. Like many of the local craftsmen I use, he is Hindu, so religion dictates when he can eat and work during the day. Often the craftsmen sit up all night working and smoking; to me there is such a sense of centre, a sense of balance or proportion."

Her unusually-shaped bracelets perfectly complement any of Sin Sin's chunky and solid rings. "Even though they are all different shapes, you can wear two or three bracelets together if you are courageous. They are heavy, solid, but they feel great on your arm."

CLOCKWISE FROM LEFT: *Square bracelet, triple-layered ring, TV ring*

Hand-made felt scarf

Meaningful MESSAGE

"With these pieces you are wearing the energy of hands, the patience of a person — as well as the timeless traditions of a noble tribe."

Creating 'wearable art' is much talked about in the world of design, but rarely executed with true panache and style. Enter Sin Sin, with her arresting hand-made felt creations that are less accessories, more sculpture, less clothing or jewellery, more adornment. "People shake their heads when I say I don't consider myself a fashion designer. But for me, singing Chinese opera, designing clothing, bags and accessories, calligraphy and traveling the world are all interconnected. They are all inspiration for my creativity. They are all a part of my life and who I am."

Renowned for her love of exotic textiles and ethnic cultures, Sin Sin was invited by German entrepeneur Christopher Gierke to visit his hidden workshop, high in the plateaus of the Outer Mongolia Orkhon Valley. Rings of traditional felt tents, or yurts, sit among stunning vistas of endless yellow grasslands, broken up by silver rivers, and herds of cashmere goats and roaming wild horses.

"There is incredible energy there, and it inspires me to make beautiful things," says Sin Sin, who re-interpreted local traditional cashmere craftsmanship to create hats, scarves, bags and coats with dramatic, sculpture-like silhouettes. She explains the simple process, which involves using only water and soap, which is rubbed by hand into the fibres. "There are no scissors or sewing involved. A pattern is created, and then the workers spin, manipulate and mould the wool into the shapes designed. With these pieces you are wearing the energy of hands, the patience of a person ... as well as the timeless traditions of a noble tribe."

"Accessories are very important, small treats you can take away. The scarf is dyed electric blue because it reminded me of the endless skies in Mongolia, but the red and white are also beautiful. I hope the pieces inspire people. Will the person wearing my jewellery, my clothing, my bags be inspired? Will I have stimulated their imagination? Will I have touched their soul? If so, my job is done."

DORA TAM

"Why follow a trend? Understand yourself and your own character: good taste is simply about making a statement that is true to who you are."

People are often surprised to discover my body of work is created by just one person: me. My whimsical, floral pieces are so different to my industrial, brushed steel collection, which is so different again to my organic, jadeite creations. One day my mood is playful, the next serious, and my jewellery reflects this. Life is short, so I experiment and explore; I try everything, and I live without regret.

I have always been unconventional. As a child I was a committed tomboy who loved climbing trees and playing in the fields, yet I also adored fairy tales, fantasy, and reading about heroes and their adventures in Greek mythology. Today I am still a dreamer, and continue to nurture that same free spirit; it can be seen in each of my creations, and it goes far beyond jewellery, to designing and painting. I am never restricted by what other people think, and I do not design with the intention of merely making money—I'm not commercial. For me, it's about the buzz of creating something new and beautiful. Art and creativity are an integral part of my life. I see myself as a sponge, soaking up my surroundings, and I am inspired by everything and anything around me. I am never confined by boundaries.

Much of my inspiration comes from watching people, getting to know them, hearing their life stories and understanding their loves and hates. I easily empathise with others, and always try to walk in their shoes, especially when I am designing a bespoke or custom-made piece. It is so important that jewellery reflects the personality of its owner. Sharing intimate information is not a typical Chinese trait; people generally build such protective boundaries, and are often scared to open up. But sharing enhances the whole experience of living. I spent several years studying and working in Canada; I love learning about different cultures, and I believe my jewellery now reflects a complex fusion of East and West, yin and yang.

I grew up in a close-knit family in the countryside, in Hong Kong, and spent my days playing with friends, and surrounded by lush, beautiful nature. While my childhood friends felt constant pressure from their parents, mine were different. I was given a lot of freedom. My parents never told me what to do, forced me into decisions, or constrained me, instead, they supported and encouraged me. We didn't have a lot of money, but even so, they did what they could to nurture my creative spirit. When I was eight, I wanted to learn the piano and for my birthday. That year, my mother bought me one; it was a huge sacrifice for her. I loved that piano and played it each day.

My mother also gave me my first piece of jewellery, a brooch in the shape of a tiny frog. As I was a tomboy, I didn't wear jewellery when I was little, but this piece was special, and I thought it was beautiful. It held a lot of meaning for me. Today, I look at jewellery as wearable art; the value of the piece doesn't come from the intrinsic worth of the gemstones, or the metal from which it is made. Instead, it comes from its artistic value, and the meaning behind it. I love the thought of passing on jewellery from generation to generation.

The pieces you choose to wear should make you feel good about yourself, and be something you really love. They are a tangible expression of who you are. I feel so lucky I can create beautiful things that make other people happy. —DT

Drama QUEEN

"I was thinking about woolly hats, flowers, the moon, and spirals."

No single piece better showcases Dora Tam's disregard of conventional design boundaries than her stunning, award-winning Diamond Tiara. "I am in love with the process of making beauty tangible, whether it's through a piece of jewellery or a painting. I look at gorgeous things and I capture them on paper, before making them real."

In 2000 Tam decided to challenge herself—and once again push her boundaries—by entering the prestigious De Beers Diamond International Award. The competition, which was held at the Louvre in Paris during Haute Couture Week, had over 2000 entrants but recognized the efforts of only 29 outstanding designers from around the globe—of which Tam was one. "The tiara, without doubt, was a turning point for me. It's certainly the most emotionally significant piece in my collection; it gave me the chance to see the world and myself in a slightly different way, and it has taken my creativity to the next level. I took a gemology introduction and jewellery making course at college in Canada, but to be honest, I enjoy the design and the wearing part much more!"

"The brief was to create a tiara, and in my head I imagined a beautiful model walking alone down a catwalk, wearing a spectacular, sparkling headpiece, illuminated by ethereal lights. I wondered how I could create a piece of dramatic jewellery that would stand out in that setting. I felt a hat would work better than a traditional tiara—actually I was thinking about woolly hats, flowers, the moon, and spirals, and somehow the design for the tiara just came together!"

Tam has a long-term working relationship with her China-based goldsmith, and both share the same design passion and ethos: he too dislikes making commercial products and prefers to create one or two perfectly engineered pieces. The collaboration between these two perfectionists produced this incredible, award-winning piece.

"This ring is based on ancient Chinese mythology."

Enchantment ring

Enchanted CIRCLE

One of Dora Tam's favourite childhood stories was a traditional Chinese tale about the Goddess Nuwa; this myth is the inspiration behind her intricate and bewitchingly delicate Enchantment Ring, made from 18-carat white gold with a 0.13-carat emerald-cut diamond.

The story goes that a great storm blew a hole in the sky and the riverbed of heaven was broken, flooding the world below. The Goddess Nuwa tried fruitlessly to plug the hole with rocks, but the stream was too strong. Eventually she collected many beautifully coloured stones from the rivers and lakes, and burned them together with reeds from the fields. For seven days and nights she kept raising the burning melted rocks to the sky, until finally the hole was filled, and the earth was safe.

"Nuwa saved the world by covering a hole in the sky, and I imagined this was the stone she used. I added the square diamond to give it sparkle; the sky was a stormy grey until Nuwa plugged it, when it became bright and beautiful once more. Because this ring is based on ancient Chinese mythology, I worked hard to ensure it had a distinctive Asian feel. It uses the traditional symbol of the circle and is flat and round, also symbolising *yin* and *yang*." Tam has chosen to use representations of flowers, leaves and twisting vines on the face of the ring, to represent the world growing once again.

"I need to spend time outside every day to feel the fresh air against my skin, and watch the tiny things in life, whether it be a bird sitting on a branch, a beetle moving through the grass, or people passing back and forth on their daily errands. I love to paint birds, flowers, anything I find to be beautiful." Tam has been an avid painter from the young age of three and has mastered pencil drawing, oils, and the intricate art of Chinese brush painting. "As I teenager I would work on one canvas for up to three months, and today I like to describe myself as a painter, a designer and an artist. When I am thinking about one particular subject, I will immerse myself totally in it. If it's fairies, I will sketch endless designs, and read fairy stories at the same time, for inspiration. If something is beautiful, I will create a piece of jewellery and a painting around that theme."

Tam's delightful paintings, which she regularly exhibits in Macau, are a contemporary and whimsical mix of bold, bright colours and girlish fantasy, often including pretty female figures and lots of blossoms and greenery.

The weight and floral pattern of the Enchantment Ring is typical of Tam's predilection towards clean-cut lines with intricate detailing. "My style is a mix of East and West, simplicity and detail, boyish yet girly, childish yet experienced somehow—multi-faceted like myself!"

Poetry & PEARLS

The inspiration for Dora Tam's ethereal pearl choker came while she was people watching at the cultural centre in Macau. "I went to see an orchestral production and I was studying the ladies coming out of the theatre. I thought they should be sweeping down the stairs wearing something elegant and dramatic. It is such a shame people no longer dress up, and that they no longer see an outing to the opera or ballet as a big event. It is a chance to play at fantasy, to wear something fantastical."

Tam's light and fairy-like pearl choker is made from silver with white gold plating and a plethora of lustrous 8mm pearls. "I like the contrast of the pearls with the silver. To me, it looks like an Elizabethan collar, something a Shakespearian heroine like Tatiana would wear."

Given its inspiration, the choker has a surprisingly modern feel. The pearls are attached to what almost looks like braided silver or chain mail. "There are hundreds of tiny links, like paper chains which my goldsmith makes by hand. It is a difficult and slow process but the end result is both sculptural and truly beautiful. The first time he made this piece he said he thought I should buy a machine to do it! To me this is a poetic and fantastical piece—wear it with a wide black or white collar."

The pearl choker forms part of Tam's Intermezzo Collection, which features a variety of bold designs incorporating pearls and silver and white gold. Intermezzo means 'between the programme' or 'intermission': "It is a very different collection, the pieces can fit anywhere and with anything. The designs vary widely from modern and pared back, to detailed and dainty like this choker."

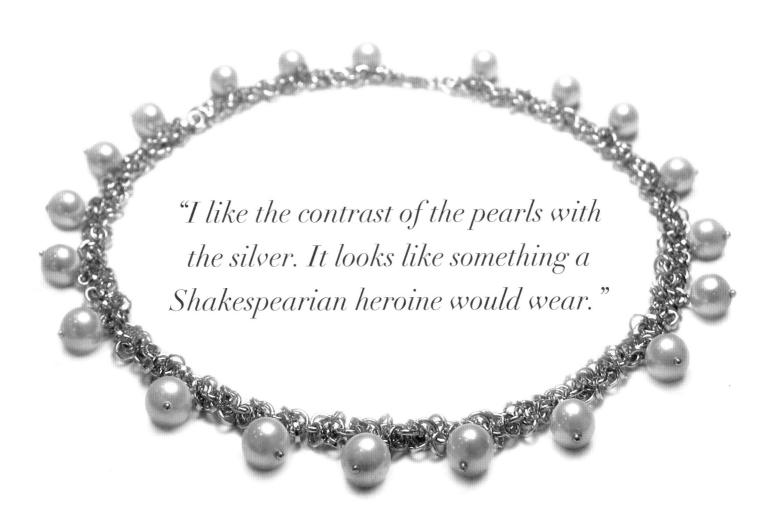

"I like the contrast of the pearls with the silver. It looks like something a Shakespearian heroine would wear."

"I deliberately created these pieces in the shape of a pebble, to capture the idea they could have been picked up from a river bed."

PRECIOUS *Pebbles*

Dora Tam is a natural communicator: a people person. So for her, designing custom-made jewellery and the process of working closely with a client, is the best part of her job. "Having someone in mind who will be wearing the pieces helps inspire my designs. That connection is so important, and if the piece or stone has a history to it, so much the better! I created something really interesting and special lately; a client gave me 13 pieces of ancient jade from a Chinese Officer's hat; that officer was her great-great-grandfather. She wanted to create a collection of jewellery she could wear today. It was my honour to help her achieve this."

The result is a stunning mixture of ancient and contemporary; Tam has used nine of the jade pieces to create a simple and strong square-shaped design that can be worn as either a brooch or a pendant. The intricately carved pieces have been laid side by side on a modern, reflective silver base and are surrounded by tiny beads, which perfectly enhance the natural luster of the jade. Tam used the remaining four pieces to create an elegant ring and earring set that complement the design of the brooch/pendant.

Tam loves to work with jadeite because of its organic shape and feel. The stones for the gorgeous pebble ring and pendant set, which were auctioned at Christies's in 2000, were sourced from a former boss in Hong Kong, who was himself an expert on jade. "I deliberately created these pieces in the shape of a pebble to give them a natural feel—I wanted to capture the idea they could have been picked up from a river bed."

"Custom-made jewellery is my passion, because I love to help people express their individual style. I begin by asking them what it is they like, they have to tell me everything. Only when I get the answers, can I start. People don't come to me because of the weight of my gold or my stones; instead, they appreciate the thought behind each creation."

BANDS
of STEEL

"The architectural cuffs in industrial brushed silver, bordered with sunset-hued spessartite, look equally good on a feminine or masculine wrist."

The creative thrust behind Dora Tam's chameleon-like style, is her desire to create jewellery that can be worn both by men and women. "We are all humans who share just the same emotions. I want to create beautiful, unisex jewellery for everyone, men as well as women. In fact, I have couples and whole families who have bought exactly the same ring for each person! It's a way of creating a bond between them."

The architectural cuffs in industrial brushed silver, bordered with sunet-hued spessartite gemstones, look equally good on a feminine or masculine wrist. Tam named them 'Eridanus', after the mythical Greek river and the starry constellation of the same name. "Following my previous collections which focused on nature and fantasy, I felt the need to break away and create something more pared-back. The silver of the cuffs is very bright and light, and contrasts with the piece's dense weight; the finish is deliberately industrial, I wanted it to look like steel."

Tam began her contemporary wedding bands design with a princess-cut diamond she found in Hong Kong. Made of 18-carat white gold, the thick bands are surprisingly comfortable to wear on the finger. "The rings are rounded inside, they 'thin out' at the side, and are fatter in the middle. I was inspired by a design I saw in Europe." In

fact, one of Tam's design gurus is Berlin-based jeweler Carl Dau, who champions the breathtakingly modern, industrial approach. "I fell in love with his work at first glance, they're all about 'less is more'. Dau's designs really spoke to me."

The Pegasus band was designed specifically for strong, independent women. The Greek translation of Pegasus is 'strong' yet simple, and Tam's interpretation of this legend is that women must be resilient and robust to achieve on so many different levels in life. Two sky-blue topaz stones are stacked within a sculptural brushed silver band, and are truly evocative of simplicity and strength.

Music, and in particular The Magic Flute opera, has been an ongoing source of inspiration in many of Tam's designs. Her Tamino cufflinks, named after the opera's prince who is in love with Pamina and has a magic flute to protect himself, are flute-inspired in both shape and design. "The small diamonds represent holes in the flute from which the music comes. I saw the opera in Macau and afterwards it came into my mind that the flute would be a great basis for cufflinks." The spirit behind the design is modern, but the fact it is based upon opera, lends it Tam's trademark whimsical air.

TRINI TAMBU

"My jewellery is unusual because it has an element of surprise. I do not limit myself; there are no rules when I design."

I grew up in Rumbai, a tiny town in the middle of the rainforest in Sumatra. Our house was cocooned by dense jungle: monkeys visited each morning to steal fruit from the trees; brightly coloured toucans squawked noisily; snakes slithered in the undergrowth, and the jungle creek was alive with fish. My mother was born and raised in Sumatra, while my father's heritage is American, British and Sri Lankan; he was expatriated by Caltex to drill for oil in the rainforest. I remember this time as one of pure happiness; we had no television, no mod cons, but it didn't matter; we'd go swimming, fishing, play basketball and baseball — it was an idyllic childhood in an exquisite place. So nature has always been a defining influence in my life, and my jewellery is a direct reflection of its beauty and wonder.

Jewellery design has always been in my blood. But surprisingly, my clearest memories of beautiful jewellery are from my father's side of the family; my paternal grandmother was the most elegant woman I have ever known. She lived between San Francisco and Kuala Lumpur and I stayed with her for a year when I was six. She had the most astonishing jewellery collection and was always exquisitely groomed. Her signature look was high heels, black pants and a head turban, accessorized with chunky pearls. She hugely influenced my style; I love pearls but equally I adore plastic pieces. I mix them all up and wear them together, I don't have to think too hard about how to put pieces with each other.

My custom-made jewellery business, Trinity Gems Bespoke, almost started by accident; it was all from word of mouth, people sought my services instead of the other way round. Making bespoke jewellery is more difficult because you have to focus on the details, and there is a lot of tweaking and fine-tuning. A fraction of a millimetre can make a big difference to the end product, and there are some things machines simply cannot produce. I am a perfectionist and for me, it is really more about quality than quantity; that is my guiding principle. It is where I want to take my creations, and how I want to be viewed: I am a designer, a creator.

I love change, and I believe it is stifling to become too comfortable in any one place or attitude. I simply look at the materials, the people, and the ideas that are presented to me at the time, and I work with them. I do not have any preconceptions. I do not flick through jewellery magazines, nor do I follow trends; my inspiration depends on whom I am designing for. It is like a spiritual process: I trust my instincts.

So I spend time getting to know a client, and then I start designing the piece in my head. Clients give you a million clues from their body language, the way they talk, dress, even how they carry themselves. I also like to paint, and when I meet a new client it is as though I see a clean canvas in my imagination. The design is created by the clues they provide during our meeting. I am a frustrated artist! I've always been attracted to art and design, and when I was young I liked to sketch all the time. I fell in love with the whole process of creating a beautiful piece of art from basically nothing. —TT

Rainforest ring

VERDANT *Jungle*

"Trini Tambu's designs communicate the intense colour, sinuous movement and the raw beauty of nature in all its complexity."

The huge, colourful and exotic Rainforest ring is an extraordinary piece. Iridescent watery light filters through the 30-carat lemon quartz stone in the centre of the ring, which is surrounded by over 200 tiny red rubies, diamonds, orange sapphires and intensely green tsavorites. One is immediately transported to the Sumatran jungle by way of the trailing vines, feathery ferns and winged insects, which twist their way up the side of the ring and embrace the centre stone. The lemon quartz is set in rhodium and black gold, echoing the dank shadows of the deepest rainforest, and contrasts with the 18-carat white gold band.

Gradation of colour is extremely important to Trini Tambu, and the defining characteristic of her jewellery. The Rainforest ring, like many of her designs, makes use of gradual and subtle layering of colour, using stones that blend from white to palest yellow, to watery greens to deepest blues. The colour builds imperceptibly from the white gold band to a riot of greens, reds, pinks and blues at the top of the ring.

"When you see a beautiful thing most people don't realize the depth and the thought process behind it," says Tambu. "It takes a lot of careful thought about colour gradation even when using diamonds, from the very clear to the slightly yellow. It took me six months to correctly place the stones, to find the right thickness of the fern, and the right size of the butterfly. The idea just came to me. I made a piece with fireflies for a client, and then decided to create another that would contain the whole jungle in a ring. I find the jungle fascinating and I wanted to encapsulate it."

Tambu says a ring of this size and grandeur must be worn with confidence, and offset by clothes that form a backdrop to the piece. "It's like having a beautiful Van Gogh painting and surrounding it with colourful clutter; the painting will lose its impact. I would wear very simple, smooth-line clothes, with perhaps small diamond stud earrings not to overpower it. You could wear jeans and a simple t-shirt, or a tailored black outfit, you could dress it up or down. Be versatile—my jewellery is designed to be very versatile. No rules!"

OCEAN Depths

The raw power and icy beauty of the ocean has inspired many of Trini Tambu's pieces. From the silvery-grey sheen of her baroque pearl and diamond drop earrings to the breathtaking 30 gram baroque pearl, blue sapphire and diamond ring, they capture the very essence of the foaming sea.

Tambu has used the soft, rounded curves of a huge gleaming baroque pearl to bring the movement and swell of the waves to life; by carefully layering tiny blue sapphires and diamonds beneath the pearl, the ring echoes the ebb and flow of the sea: "The minute I saw the baroque pearl at a Japanese dealer, I knew I had to have it—and I knew exactly what I was going to do with it. I wanted to communicate the idea of the ocean, without disrupting the natural curve of the pearl. So I carefully placed tendrils of white gold encrusted with diamonds on top—how appropriate, the water playing off the surface, the spray washing off the pearl!" But this level of perfection takes patience and time; Tambu spent hours playing with the mould that would encase the final ring and with the lie of the white gold tendrils to ensure they closely hugged the surface of the pearl. "I had to carefully choose the colours and the grade of each stone at the base of the ring, to get a tiered effect from dark to light that reflects the ocean. The sapphires and diamonds are set in white gold and edged with black rhodium which waves up and down all around the pearl; if it were set in regular white gold it would look totally different. With this setting the depth of the ocean is captured in the ring."

Tambu has a huge collection of loose pearls; they are one of her favourite materials to design with. She chose to pair two shimmering south sea baroque pearls with 20 small articulated diamonds to create elegant 18 carat white gold drop earrings; clearly reflecting her signature style of natural, raw beauty. "I work a lot with baroque pearls, because they are very irregular, and I love that no two are exactly the same. There's no uniformity. I wanted the focus of this piece to be the pearls, and the diamonds do not detract from their natural lustre, but simply enhance it." As with much of Tambu's jewellery, the earrings are specifically designed so they can be worn in several different ways. The top of the earring is a white gold loop, which can be attached to plain studs, to a diamond loop, or simply just a pearl, each giving a different effect. Tambu says the earrings are strong pieces designed to be worn on their own, without a necklace, but can be paired with a simple bracelet or ring for maximum impact.

The freshwater pearl and 18 carat gold necklace is a versatile piece that can be worn everyday, or dressed up for evening: "It's very simple and understated, but you can also hook on a big baroque pearl to dress the necklace up a little," says Tambu. No matter which of these pieces you wear, you are immediately reminded of the sea.

"I love and am fascinated by the ocean; it is an unknown, there's so much to discover, a totally different world. I am attracted by its sense of mystery, and it is this that I have tried to emulate in these pieces of jewellery."

"I am fascinated by the ocean, and attracted by its sense of mystery."

Baroque pearl necklace and drop earrings; baroque pearl ring

Natural WONDERS

The coiling green of a jungle creeper, the foaming crash of a wave, and the coral-encrusted reef are all evocatively captured in these three rings, showing just how important and influential nature is to Trini Tambu.

Tambu's childhood spent in the jungles of south east Asia has left her with an enduring love of intense colour and soft, sinous lines; the 18 carat white gold, diamond, and tsavorite leaf ring brilliantly captures the wild beauty of the jungle in a simple and understated way. The cleverly designed ring is actually two separate pieces that fit together like a corkscrew; it is possible to wear the pieces separately, or twist them together to make one ring that snakes up the finger, like a jungle creeper. "At the time I was experimenting with non-traditional, funky styles, I was interested to see how people would react." says Tambu. "This is a one of a kind piece. The soft lines give movement, and the curves of each shape fit perfectly into each other. It's not overly fussy or intricate, it's actually a very simple, structured yet feminine ring. When you twist it apart, the piece covered with tiny brown diamonds fits on the bottom part of your finger and can be worn everyday."

The starfish ring takes you straight to the watery depths of a reef, with its barnacle encrusted rocks and shimmering coral. "I was experimenting with purple; I was sorting out stones and I noticed the purple gradation on the sapphires," says Tambu. "I also had some amethysts, and I thought it would be nice to combine them. My workman was horrified! He said you can't combine precious and semi-precious stones! But I believe the results speak for themselves." Tambu's inspiration came from a holiday spent in Sulawesi, Indonesia, where she did a lot of snorkeling. "It's unbelievable to me that only 50m from the beach,

there's a totally different world. Nature holds the secret to how we should combine colours, it's all around us with such intensity." The gemstones gradually grade from pink to purple, and the texture of the coloured stones lends the ring a sandy feel, together with the coarse and bumpy appearance of a starfish. Each arm of the starfish is lined with a delicate strip of white gold, giving greater definition to the piece. "I like starfish!" says Tambu. "I like the way they mould to wherever they are; my starfish wraps around the ring. This ring is about shapes, shapes that hug other shapes; it's about layering, and the colour is layered too. The back of the ring has been designed to look like the ocean bed, like sand, with starfish sitting on it. I always try to do something different on the underside of my jewellery, it makes it more exciting to wear if you're the only person who knows there's something extra underneath! Despite the rich detail and the vivid colours, Tambu says this is a ring that can be worn everyday with jeans, or dressed up for a special event.

A multitude of yellow sapphires and white diamonds make up the undulating curves of Tambu's pave set wave ring; it is strongly reminiscent of a wave's foamy skirt traveling across the golden sand. "When I made this five years ago, it was an unusual setting. No one else was trying to add movement into the setting of rings this size. I think the movement makes it more interesting, it's not just one shape. Once again my inspiration came from water, think of how a stone creates a ripple effect when you throw it into the water. I've tried to suggest this in the setting." Tambu has always loved yellow, and has used the lighter-coloured stones to give the large ring a daintiness. "Yellow is the sunset; it's a happy colour, and one I love to use in my designs."

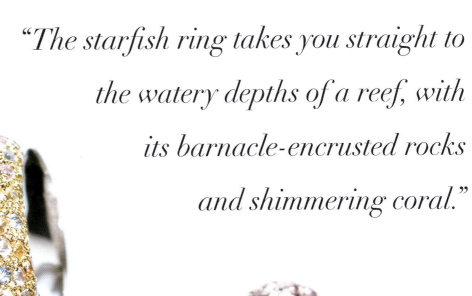

"The starfish ring takes you straight to the watery depths of a reef, with its barnacle-encrusted rocks and shimmering coral."

Coral BLUSH

Swimming through the brightly coloured, undulating coral reefs of Thailand, Trini Tambu was struck by how cleverly nature combines colours and textures, in patterns and hues even an artist might not put together. Inspired, she started sketching immediately, and set about creating two unusual rings mimicking the flower-beds and sea plants of the ocean as they are pulled at by the current. In these pieces, the stones are silkily smooth and rounded, and yet the overall effect is one of rough movement and texture.

The first ring combines different sized stones of intense blue turquoise with two lustrous white South Sea pearls, and a multitude of tiny red rubies, all set in 18 carat yellow gold. "I made this several years ago; I hadn't seen anyone using turquoise with south sea pearls in quite this manner. It's an unusual combination," says Tambu. "When the ring sits on your finger it sticks up and out; almost as if it's three dimensional. I took a long time over the design because with a ring of this size, it's important to make sure it is comfortable and not too high, but it had to be high enough to create the look and feel of a coral flower. I personally think the piece has a Middle Eastern feel, and strangely enough, the lady who bought it was from the Middle East!"

The coral theme continues with the second ring, but the colour palette is more subtle; instead of turquoise, Tambu used tiny diamonds with the rubies and different coloured pearls to create a softer piece. "Pearls come in many different hues and undertones—white on white, grey, yellow, pink—so it was a challenge to find the right pearls with yellowish undertones that would tie the ring together," says Tambu. "The diamonds lighten the piece up; with such a large ring that is meant to emulate coral, you certainly don't want it to look or feel heavy or cumbersome! Instead, it's a big ring that sits out from your hand, but looks surprisingly delicate."

Tambu says she finds the mystery of the ocean endlessly compelling, but she also draws inspiration from beautiful colour photographs in illustrated nature books. "The nice thing about this ring is that you can wear it casually, but equally you can go to a black tie function and wear it with a glamorous dress, and it will look beautiful. Now more than ever, jewellery is not jewellery per se; it has been translated into a fashion statement. You can wear something as a belt, you can pin it in your hair, you can use it as a brooch. A piece is not always used in its traditional sense, and people are very adventurous now, which is great to see. The media bombards us with what they think is good and what's in right now, but what looks good on real people can sometimes be quite different! So I think you have to understand your degree of confidence and what you like as a person, follow your heart when you're choosing jewellery, and don't just buy a piece because it's the 'in' thing!"

"The rings mimick the ocean's
flower-beds and sea plants as they
are pulled by the currents."

Tahitian pearl bobble ring and necklace

GRACEFUL

Curves

To Trini Tambu, the shapes, hues and movement of organic objects are perfection in themselves. So the inspiration behind this ring and necklace set was simply taken from the graceful curve of a natural Tahitian pearl; Tambu has recreated its soft lines and arcs, using brightly coloured sapphires and rubies.

"When you design you want to be creative, so it's sometimes easy to miss the basic shapes of nature; at the time I made this set, nobody had thought of making a pearl-shaped ball in different coloured gems. The Tahitian pearls have a peacock-coloured undertone, they have a bluish-greenish tinge, which is perfectly offset by the coloured balls. In fact, the coloured balls reflect the natural lustre of the pearl. Once you put the colours together, everything falls into place, it's like the layers of paint that make up a masterpiece. You might see a green background in a painting, but there are actually a great many colours beneath the surface that build up the depth, and give the overall effect."

Tambu has given the ring an unusual twist by encrusting the front section of the band with the same blue sapphires that stud the blue pearl-shaped ball. "I used grey gold and black rhodium to accentuate the pearls and gems, and then put the blue stones around the band to create a natural flow that is more pleasing to the eye. The blue-encrusted band

carries the eye down and around the ring. I purposefully design so that all the elements come together smoothly, even though the colours and textures are so different. It's similar to when you have lots of different pictures and you want to put them on one wall. If you frame each one in the same way, it holds the collection together."

The accompanying necklace has a fluid movement of its own. "Every girl has a pearl necklace, but I wanted to create something slightly different. I combined Tahitian pearls with colourful, studded pearl-shaped balls; I've arranged them in a way that creates movement and flow in the necklace. It's interesting to combine different colours, dark blue with dark red together are always classic colour combinations, and the white softens the red. Pearls work with almost anything; they can be designed to look funky, not traditional. So while this is a pearl necklace, it's bigger and heavier than your average strand: the pearls are around 3 grams each, with a diameter of 2.8cm. You could add it to your regular string of pearls for an even more unusual, eye-catching piece of jewellery."

Tambu believes pearls complement most skin tones, and can significantly brighten anyone's complexion. "Pearls reflect light onto the face; you just have to find the right pearl and look for you. Trust your instincts. When something is beautiful, it falls into place effortlessly!"

Contacts

Sandra d'Auriol
SANDRA@DAURIOL.COM

Cindy Chao
WWW.CINDYCHAO.COM

Sandrine Clayton
WWW.CLAYTONX.COM.HK

Jean-François Fichot
WWW.JF-F.COM

Wynn Wynn Ong
WWW.NAGAJEWELRY.COM

Tayma Page Allies
WWW.TAYMAJEWELLERY.COM

Toni Patrizio
WWW.CULTURESBYTONIP.COM

Sin Sin
WWW.SINSIN.COM.HK

Dora Tam
WWW.DORATAMDESIGN.COM

Trini Tambu
WWW.TRINITYGEMSBESPOKE.COM

HIDDEN
GEMS of
ASIA